P9-CMK-726

TRUE STORIES OF
THE SECOND
WORLD WAR

First published in 2003 by Usborne Publishing Ltd,
Usborne House, 83-85 Saffron Hill,
London EC1N 8RT, England.
www.usborne.com

Copyright © 2003 Usborne Publishing Ltd.
U.E. First published in America in 2003.

The name Usborne and the devices ♀ 🌐 are Trade Marks
of Usborne Publishing Ltd. All rights reserved. No part of
this publication may be reproduced, stored in a retrieval system
or transmitted in any form or by any means, electronic,
mechanical, photocopying, recording or otherwise, without
the prior permission of the publisher.

A catalogue record for this title is available
from the British Library.

ISBN 07945 05996

Printed in Great Britain

Designed by Sarah Cronin
Illustrated by Jeremy Gower and Kuo Kang Chen
Series editors: Jane Chisholm and Rosie Dickins
Series designer: Mary Cartwright
With thanks to Georgina Andrews
Cover photograph © Fox Photos/Getty Images
Cover design by Glen Bird

With grateful thanks to Terry Charman, of the Imperial War Museum,
London, for his most helpful comments on the manuscript.

TRUE STORIES OF
THE SECOND
WORLD WAR

Paul Dowswell

HA CASS COUNTY PUBLIC LIBRARY
400 E. MECHANIC
HARRISONVILLE, MO 64701

0 0022 0444801 9

CONTENTS

"As dirty a business as the world has ever seen..."

More than half a century now separates us from the Second World War. The number of films, TV documentaries and books still produced on the subject show that it continues to exert a powerful fascination. Today the numbers of those who actually fought in the war is rapidly dwindling, but many people have grandparents or other relations who remember it all too well as children. The conflict is not some distant history – it is still within graspable, living memory.

The stories in this book touch on many different aspects of the war. There are epic naval encounters between titanic warships, and monumental battles between armies of hundreds of thousands of men. But there are also single-handed duels between opposing snipers, and other tales of lonely individuals facing almost certain death.

For those who survived the war it would remain the most intense and vivid experience of their lives. Many of those who died were in their late teens or early twenties – and many of them would still be alive today had the war not come to scythe them away.

The Second World War was fought between two great power blocs. On one side was the Axis – an alliance of Germany, Italy and Japan, who were also joined by Hungary, Romania and Bulgaria. On the other side were the Allies – principally Britain and her empire, Soviet Russia and the United States. These gargantuan forces faced off against each other in four major areas of fighting: Western Europe, Eastern Europe and the U.S.S.R, North Africa, and the Eastern Pacific and South East Asia (see maps on pages 9 and 10).

The cause of any war is usually too complex to reduce to a simple explanation. But, in essence, World War Two was caused by the desire of the Axis powers to gain empires and the unwillingness of the Allies to let them. Nazi dictator Adolf Hitler dreamed of *lebensraum* (living space) in Eastern Europe and Russia, for his German master race. Mussolini wanted to create a new Roman empire for Italy. Japan's military rulers sought to take over the Asian and Pacific territories fading European powers had seized for their own empires in previous centuries.

The war began with the German invasion of Poland on September 1, 1939. Here Polish cavalry charged against German tanks with predictably disastrous results. It ended on September 2, 1945, six years and a day later, when Japan finally surrendered, following the destruction of two of her cities by atomic bombs. At first Germany and her allies made

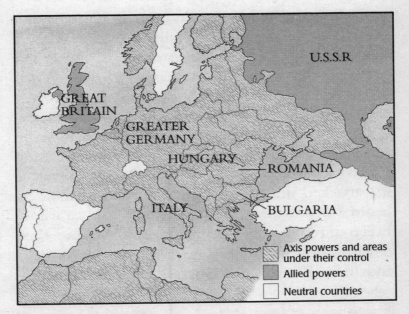

The balance of power in Europe, October/November 1942.

spectacular advances, and almost all of Europe fell under their control. This was largely due to the effective fighting strength of the German army and their *Blitzkrieg* (lightning war) tactics. Here, tanks, aircraft and other powered vehicles, were used to make fast and highly effective work of opposing armies. In the first two years of the war, only Britain held out, protected from an invasion by its air force, navy and the English Channel. The Battle of Britain - the first significant aerial battle in history - was Hitler's first defeat.

With Britain isolated at the edge of the continent, Hitler turned to his chief ambition, the conquest of

"As dirty a business..."

Soviet Russia. The invasion on June 22, 1941, was the greatest in history. By the autumn of that year, German troops were at the gates of Leningrad and Moscow. But a suicidal resistance by Red Army troops, and the onset of the ferocious Russian winter, prevented Hitler from snatching his greatest prize.

On the other side of the world, Germany's ally Japan had been establishing her own empire on the Asian Pacific seaboard (see map). On December 7, she attacked the United States at Pearl Harbor. So began a devastating campaign, which saw her armies sweep through the Philippines and Malaya, then down to Java and Burma, to threaten both Australia and India. When Japan attacked the United States,

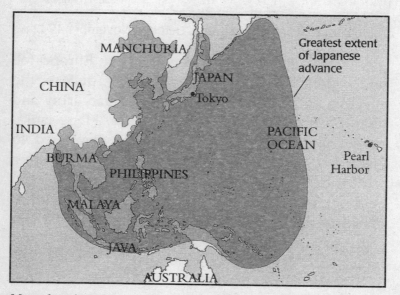

Map showing the greatest extent of the Japanese advance

Hitler also declared war on the Americans, despite the fact that he had still to defeat the British and the Russians. British prime minister Winston Churchill was ecstatic. "So we had won the war after all. Our history would not come to an end," he reflected that night. "Hitler's fate was sealed... As for the Japanese, they would be ground to a powder. All the rest was merely the proper application of overwhelming force."

He was absolutely right. Germany and Japan had decided to wage war against the most powerful nation on Earth. America responded to their challenge by diverting her vast industrial strength to winning the war. In three and a half years, her dockyards built 1,200 new warships. By 1944, her factories were producing one new warplane every five minutes. Quite aside from this mammoth expenditure, $2 billion was still found to fund the development of the world's first atomic weapons.

In the summer of 1942, American, British and Commonwealth troops began to claw back territory seized by Japan in the first six months of the Pacific war. In North Africa, a British victory against German and Italian troops at El Alamein, in October 1942, scotched any possibility that German and Japanese troops would link up in India. The victory also allowed for the American and British invasion of Italy from the south, which took place in July 1943.

During 1942, the Soviets began to recover from the invasion of 1941. Their armies were better

11

equipped, both from their own factories and substantial American and British arms imports, and their soldiers had become a formidable fighting force. When Russian troops destroyed the German 6th Army at Stalingrad over the winter of 1942 to 1943, the war in the east turned into a slow retreat that ended with the Soviet occupation of the German capital, Berlin.

On June 6, 1944, American, British and Canadian troops took part in the D-Day landings in Normandy. Now Hitler's armies had to fight on three fronts – Eastern Europe, Western Europe and Italy. Within a year the war in Europe was over. Hitler committed suicide on April 30, 1945, and on May 8 Germany surrendered. Japan lasted through to the summer, until the devastating atomic bomb attacks on Hiroshima and Nagasaki.

Novelist John Steinbeck's description of the war: "As dirty a business as the world has ever seen..." seems a fair epitaph. At least fifty-five million people died as a direct result of it.

The first and final voyage of the *Bismarck*

The war at sea, May 1941

In early May of 1941, the crew of the *Bismarck* had been feverishly preparing for an inspection by none other than the German *führer* (leader), Adolf Hitler. Now he was here among them. Decks had been scrubbed, rails polished, uniforms pressed and the ship's barber had worked his way through as many of the 2,100 men as time and his blistered fingers allowed. The visit to Germany's greatest battleship was going well. The crew, whose average age was all of 21, were immensely proud of their new vessel. As Hitler passed their assembled ranks, they stood there, faces stiff with pride and overawed to be in the presence of their leader. Not everyone on parade was impressed with Hitler, though. As he walked by anti-aircraft gunner Alois Haberditz, the Nazi leader looked straight through him. Haberditz shuddered. Hitler had eyes as cold and pitiless as a shark.

The Führer, who had an almost schoolboy fascination with battleships, was taken on a tour of the ship. He seemed particularly interested in the

The first and final voyage of the *Bismarck*

Bismarck's gunnery control system – a state-of-the-art computer mechanism which took in the ship's speed and course and that of its enemy, wind direction and shell flight time. This produced changes of correction of aim at what was – by the standards of the time – lightning speed. Hitler also noted with pride the two huge swastikas – the emblem of his Nazi party – painted at either end of the ship, which served to identify it to their own aircraft.

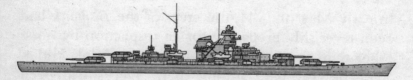

Germany's greatest battleship, the *Bismarck*

Germany had a small navy, but her warships were the most advanced in the world, and the *Bismarck* was the pride of her fleet. A truly gargantuan war machine, over one quarter of a km (one sixth of a mile) long, and bristling with huge guns, she was unquestionably the fastest and best armed and protected battleship of her day.

Among the officials with Hitler on this tour of inspection were *Bismarck*'s two most senior officers. The Captain was Ernst Lindemann, a stiff, rather frail looking 45-year-old, who was never seen without a cigarette. In his official portrait, Lindemann stares out at the world with piercing, intelligent eyes, his blond hair slicked back on his head, with two enormous ears. But his stern and slightly comical look was misleading. His crew held him in both high regard and affection – some even referred to him respectfully as "our father". He emanated both approachability and confidence, and being appointed captain of the *Bismarck* was the greatest break in his naval career.

Also sent to sea with Lindemann was the fleet commander, Admiral Günther Lütjens, together with 50 of his staff. Lütjens was a starkly handsome 51-year-old, bearing a passing resemblance to American film actor Lee Marvin. Lütjens, like Lindemann and many officers in the German navy, was not a great supporter of Hitler, and had tried to protect Jewish officers under his command. Right from the start of the war he had believed Germany would be defeated. Perhaps that was why he was such a forbidding man to be around, and it was said that he almost never smiled or laughed. Although he was a fine and experienced commander, he did not have Lindemann's leadership skills, as subsequent events would show. Lütjens knew the British feared his powerful ship, and that they would do everything in their considerable power to destroy it. He, more than any man aboard the *Bismarck*, did not expect to return from this posting alive.

At this stage of the war, Britain was the only major European power still undefeated by the Nazis. Hitler, and Germany's commander-in-chief of the navy,

The first and final voyage of the *Bismarck*

Grand Admiral Erich Raeder, intended to use the navy to starve their isolated island opponent into defeat. Britain's survival, after all, depended on cargo ships from her colonies and North America. So far this tactic was working. In early 1941, the battleships *Scharnhorst* and *Gneisenau* had ventured out into the North Atlantic on raiding missions and sunk 22 merchant ships between them. Now, in May of this year, the *Bismarck* was preparing to do the same. The expedition was code named *Rheinübung* ("Operation Rhine"), and sailing out with the *Bismarck* was another modern ship, the *Prinz Eugen*. This raid would be different. On previous missions German warships had been told to avoid battle with the British Navy at all cost, and concentrate solely on destroying merchant ships. But now, so confident were the officers of the German High Command in their new warships, they had given permission for them to fight back if they came under attack.

Most of the crew, in their invincible youth and invincible battleship, had no idea of the horrors that awaited them. But a few more experienced ones had been aboard sinking ships, and were old enough to know that the British Navy was actually quite a formidable foe. Even Grand Admiral Raeder had admitted to confidants that the surface vessels in his navy (as opposed to his lethally effective submarine fleet) could do no more than take part in hit and run raids. They were heavily outnumbered by the British, who had always depended on their powerful fleet to keep control of their sprawling overseas empire and protect their trade. When Raeder heard that war had broken out with Britain, he greeted the news with resignation. "Our surface forces can do no more than show that they can die gallantly," he declared.

Almost from the start of their mission, *Bismarck* and *Prinz Eugen* were shadowed by British planes and ships – all carefully keeping out of range of their powerful guns. When news reached the British Admiralty that the two German ships had left Korsfjord, in Norway, to venture out into the shipping lanes of the North Atlantic, immediate action was taken. The Royal Navy ordered two of their own most powerful warships – *Hood* and *Prince of Wales* – to intercept them, and these ships slipped away from their Orkney base at Scapa Flow in the early hours of May 22. In overall command of this force was Vice-Admiral Lancelot Holland, who sailed aboard the *Hood*. A grey-haired, distinguished-looking man, he had the air of a venerable BBC commentator wheeled out to present a royal funeral. Within a day, another great battleship, *King George V*, the aircraft carrier *Victorious*, and four cruisers, had also set off to join him.

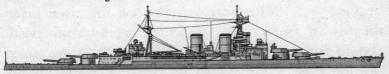

The British Royal Navy's ill-fated *Hood*

The first and final voyage of the *Bismarck*

The *Hood* was quite possibly the most famous battle cruiser in the world. Built in 1918, she was a handsome and formidably-armed vessel, a sixth of a mile from bow to stern. *Hood* had become a symbol of British naval power, and had a fearsome reputation. During training exercises, the crew of the *Bismarck* had frequently run through attack and resistance tactics, with *Hood* as their imaginary enemy. Now they were about to fight her for real.

Bismarck and *Prinz Eugen* took a course up past the north of Iceland, and through the Denmark Straits, which separate Iceland from Greenland. Here they sailed close by the huge sheath of ice which forms around the coastal waters of Greenland for most of the year. On the journey up, the two deck swastikas were hurriedly covered over with a fresh coat of paint. The only aircraft out here would be British ones – and such insignia would clearly indicate that the *Bismarck* was an enemy ship. It was in these chilly waters that the *Hood* and the *Prince of Wales* raced to intercept them.

This far north, during spring and summer, night falls for a few hours or not at all. In late May, dawn came before 2:00am, casting a pale grey light over a heaving sea, dotted by patches of fog and brief flurries of snow. Men stationed in lookout posts aboard the ships longed to scuttle back to the cozy fug of their cramped quarters, as a biting wind gnawed at their bones, and icy spray whipped over the bows to sting their numb faces. This desolate spot near the frozen top of the world was one of the most dismal places on Earth.

Aboard the German ships, crews were expecting an imminent attack. But they had no real idea how close the British actually were. The cruiser *Suffolk* had sighted them just after 11:00 in the evening on May 23. Alerted, Vice-Admiral Holland closed in at once. By 5:00 the next morning, he was expecting to sight his enemy at any minute. Sure enough, two ships were spotted at 5:30am, black dots 27km (17 miles) away on their northwest horizon.

On *Bismarck* and *Prinz Eugen*, the crews had spent an anxious night. There had been several false alarms as hydrophone (sound detection) operators thought they had picked up the incoming rumble of British engines. But it was a radio message from German headquarters, who had been monitoring British transmissions, that told them their enemy was almost upon them. Just after the message arrived, lookouts spotted two smoke trails from the funnels of the approaching British, on the southeast horizon. Even then, the Germans were not sure this was an attack. Perhaps they were still being shadowed by smaller vessels, who were just keeping tabs on them.

But by 5:50am it was obvious to Lütjens that the approaching ships meant to attack him. He sent a terse radio message to his headquarters: "Am engaging two heavy ships." Then he prepared himself for the battle to come.

The first and final voyage of the *Bismarck*

In all four ships, in an oft-rehearsed procedure, one ton high-explosive shells were hauled up to the huge gun turrets by a complex system of pulleys and rails from magazines deep inside the hull. In *Bismarck* and *Hood*, these monstrous projectiles were 38 or 41cm (15 or 16 inches) across, and were loaded into guns 6m (20ft) long and weighing 100 tons each.

Holland gave the order to open fire at 21km (13 miles), and almost at once all four ships began exchanging broadsides. At these distances shells would take up to half a minute to reach their target. It was just before 6:00am. So loud was the roar of their huge guns they could be heard in Reykjavik, the capital of Iceland. But when battle began it soon became apparent that the *Hood*'s reputation had been undeserved.

Built just after the First World War, she had been given heavy steel protection along her vertical surfaces - when current warship designs assumed enemy shells would travel in low and hit her sides. Twenty years later, such assumptions no longer applied. By 1940 warships aimed their shells in high, arc-like trajectories, where they plunged down on top of decks and turrets. Here were *Hood*'s weakest spots. And the *Bismarck*'s second and third salvo had an astonishing effect on the British ship. Men aboard *Bismarck* and *Prinz Eugen* watched in astonishment as their much-feared opponent exploded like a giant firework, lifting the entire front half up out of the water, and breaking the battleship in two. A huge, strangely silent sheet of flame shot high in the air, as intense as a blow torch and so bright it could be seen over 50km (30 miles) away. *Hood* turned over and sank. In less than five minutes, in the bleakest of battlegrounds, Vice-Admiral Holland and all but three of his 1,421 crew died.

Prince of Wales veered sharply to avoid hitting the *Hood*. She was in deep trouble herself. Seven shells from *Prinz Eugen* and *Bismarck* had hit her, including one at the bridge which had killed everyone there but the Captain, John Leach, and two of his officers. Several of her main gun turrets had also jammed. Sensing another catastrophe, and with no chance of destroying either German ship, Leach ordered a speedy retreat.

Aboard the *Bismarck* and *Prinz Eugen* there was an atmosphere of euphoria. The crews had been led to believe they were aboard the most powerful warships on the planet, and events had proved this to be true. Hadn't they? Yet the atmosphere on *Bismarck's* bridge was strained. Lütjens and Lindemann had exchanged sharp words about the wisdom of going after the *Prince of Wales*. Even though she was an easy target, Lütjens had decided to stick to his original mission – sinking enemy merchant ships. He was not prepared to take any unnecessary risks.

And there was bad news too. Although *Prinz Eugen* had escaped unscathed, *Bismarck* had taken two shells from the *Prince of Wales*. Men had been killed and the ship's medical bay was filling up with burned and scalded casualties. Most serious of all, a shell had sailed clean through the front of the ship close to the bow. It had not exploded, but had left a man-sized hole, just above the water line. As the *Bismarck* lurched up and down through the choppy ocean, the sea flooded in and drained out, gradually filling the surrounding compartments with 2,000 tons of water. Fuel lines had been broken, leaving 1,000 tons of fuel in the forward tanks cut off from the engine room, and the ship was seeping a sickly brown trail of oil. Part of the ship's engine had also been damaged.

News of the *Hood*'s destruction caused a sensation across the world. British prime minister Winston Churchill would recall it as the single worst moment of the war. The British Admiralty issued a famous order "SINK THE *BISMARCK*", and four battleships, two battle cruisers, two aircraft carriers, 13 cruisers, and 21 destroyers were dispatched to avenge the *Hood*. The man given the responsibility of hunting down the *Bismarck* was Admiral John Tovey, commander of the British home fleet. A small, dapper man, whose sharp, determined features gave him something of the look of a bull terrier, Tovey had considerable forces at his disposal, including his own flagship *King George V*.

Tovey's first task was to ensure the *Bismarck* did not vanish from sight. The North Atlantic, after all, stretched for more than a million nautical square miles. Although she was still being shadowed by smaller British vessels, it would be easy enough to lose her.

On the morning of *Bismarck*'s first extraordinary day in action, the rain and drizzle eventually gave way to an occasional hint of sunshine, but the sea was still heaving. Lütjens and Lindemann had been considering their options. Their ship was losing fuel and taking in water. Although it still had full firepower, it now lacked speed – an essential attribute for its hit and run mission. Lütjens ordered the *Prinz Eugen* to break away from *Bismarck* and continue alone. He would take his own ship back to the port of St. Nazaire, France, for repairs. At their current speed, they should make the 2,700km (1,700 mile) journey in just under four days.

Meanwhile, the British made their first counterattack with *Swordfish* torpedo bombers from the aircraft carrier *Victorious*. These quaint biplanes looked like relics from the First World War, and they lumbered dangerously slowly through the sky. *Bismarck* fought off the *Swordfish* with ease – her AA (anti-aircraft) guns putting up a protective sheet of flame that prevented the planes from launching their torpedoes accurately. There was one hit, but it caused minimal damage. But, far to the south, another British aircraft carrier was hurrying up to intercept the *Bismarck*. The *Ark Royal*, and her *Swordfish* crews would soon prove to be far more deadly.

The first and final voyage of the *Bismarck*

Sunday May 25 was Lütjens birthday. He had always believed he would die on this mission, and had resigned himself to the fact that this would be his last ever birthday. That midday he made a speech to his men – talking to them over the ship's PA system – and something of his dark mood rubbed off on a crew still exuberant from their brush with the *Hood* and *Prince of Wales*.

"The *Hood* was the pride of England," he told them. "The enemy will now attempt to concentrate his forces and set them on to us... The German nation is with you. We will fight till our gun barrels glow red and the last shell has left the breech. For us soldiers it is now 'victory or death'."

It was not a diplomatic choice of words – but even admirals are human, and Lütjens knew all too well what was coming. But he was too pessimistic. During the night of May 25 *Bismarck* had outrun her British pursuers, and when dawn came they had lost sight of her. But Lütjens did not know this. Later that day he sent a long, despondent message to German High Command. This was picked up by British radio trackers, who concentrated an aerial search in the area where they detected the signal. But even then, luck was still with Lütjens. Tovey's fleet miscalculated his position – and assumed *Bismarck* was heading back to Norway, rather than France. They altered their own pursuit course accordingly.

It would be a whole 31 hours before the British

The first and final voyage of the *Bismarck*

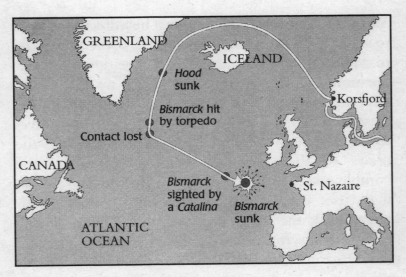

GREENLAND

ICELAND

Hood sunk

Bismarck hit by torpedo

Contact lost

Korsfjord

CANADA

Bismarck sighted by a *Catalina*

Bismarck sunk

St. Nazaire

ATLANTIC OCEAN

The last voyage of the *Bismarck*, May 1941

found the *Bismarck*. Around 10:30 on the morning of May 26, observant members of the crew noticed an RAF *Catalina* flying boat circling just outside the range of their AA guns. By now the ailing battleship was approaching the Bay of Biscay. The port of St. Nazaire was a mere day or so away, as was the imminent prospect of both U-boat and air escort. *Bismarck*'s position was duly reported by the *Catalina*, and Tovey's fleet altered course.

To the south the carrier *Ark Royal* was closing in fast, its huge bulk heaving alarmingly in the rough sea. Amid torrents of seawater that sprayed the flight deck, ground crews prepared the ponderous *Swordfish* bombers, loading heavy torpedoes onto their undersides. In the middle of the afternoon, 15

Swordfish lumbered into the air. They did not expect to sink the *Bismarck*, but they hoped, at the very least, to cause enough damage to slow her down, so that pursuing British warships could catch up and attack. Slipping through low cloud, fog and driving rain, they pounced, flying just above the churning waves to unleash their torpedoes toward their target. If the crews of the *Swordfish* were surprised by the complete lack of defensive fire from the ship below, it did not cause them to pause and consider their target. All the torpedoes missed – which was fortunate for the *Swordfish* crews, because the ship they had actually attacked was the British cruiser *Sheffield*.

Amid huge humiliation and embarrassment, a second wave of 15 *Swordfish* was sent off into the slow falling dusk. This time, they found the *Bismarck*, still 1,000km (620 miles) from St. Nazaire. They moved so slowly they seemed to be hanging in the air. But they flew in so low, their wheels almost brushing the waves, that *Bismarck*'s guns could only fire above them. This time two torpedoes hit home. One caused only minor damage. The other went off underneath the stern, with a huge watery explosion that shot like a whiplash through the length of the ship. It buckled deck plates and bulkheads, and threw men to the floor or against metal partitions and instruments, with breathtaking violence. Above the site of the explosion, water surged into the ship with a vengeance, flooding the entire steering compartment. The sea burst through once waterproof compartments. It gushed down cable pipes that ran the length of the ship, to spurt out unexpectedly, far away from the site of the damage.

Aboard the *Ark Royal*, senior commanders listened to the wildly excited reports of their young pilots, and tried to sift fact from fiction to determine exactly what damage had been done. One pilot's account seemed to indicate something extremely significant. After the attack, the *Bismarck* had been seen to make two huge circles on her course, then slow down almost to a halt. Clearly, her steering had been badly damaged. In fact, the rudder had jammed at 15° to port.

Aboard the stricken vessel desperate measures were called for. The *Bismarck* carried three seaplanes. Plans were made to remove the hangar door where they were stored, and weld it to the side of the stern, to counteract the effect of the rudder. But bad weather made such a scheme impossible.

Following the *Swordfish* attack, Lütjens sent another grim signal home: "Ship no longer steering." German naval authorities reacted by ordering U-boats to head for the *Bismarck*'s position as soon as possible. But U-boats are not the swiftest of vessels, and there were none nearby. Informed of the *Bismarck*'s grim predicament, Hitler had a radio signal sent to Lütjens: "All of Germany is with you. What can still be done will be done. The performance of your duty will strengthen our people in their struggle for their existence." It was not a message that offered any hope of survival.

Bismarck's crew passed a long, dreadful night – each man wondering whether he would live to see another dusk. Many had nightmares, and men woke screaming or sobbing. When word spread that the rudder had been put out of action, the older members of the crew took this to be a death sentence. Later in the night, permission was given for the crew to help themselves to anything they wanted – food, drink – a tacit admission that the ship was doomed. But Lindemann had assured them U-boats and aircraft were heading out to protect them, and some of the younger sailors still held out hope that they would survive after all.

During the night, Lindemann ordered the engines to stop. When the chief engineer requested they be started again, Lindemann replied, "Ach, do as you like." After five nights with virtually no sleep, and all the stress and worry of commanding a ship in a now impossible situation, he was a man at the end of his tether.

To keep the crew from brooding overmuch about the battle to come, records of popular songs were played over the ship's PA system. But such obvious psychological tactics failed – the songs reminded the men too much of girlfriends or wives and families back home. Lindemann had also come up with the ruse of getting men with no immediate job to do to construct a dummy funnel of wood and canvas. The idea was to change the *Bismarck's* silhouette, so that enemy ships or aircraft would think it was another battleship, and leave it alone. This was some considerable task, and men were kept busy painting the canvas and building the scaffolding structure right through the day.

At first light on May 27, the day *Bismarck* had hoped to reach the safety of a French port, Tovey and his fleet closed in to finish the job. Along with his own flagship *King George V*, was the huge battleship *Rodney*, the cruisers *Norfolk* and *Dorsetshire*, and several others.

Aboard the *Bismarck,* exhausted lookouts saw two massive ships heading straight for them. Tovey intended the sight of *King George V* and *Rodney* boldly closing in to unnerve the German crew, and it worked. The battle that followed, which started with a salvo from *Rodney* at 8:47am, was unspeakably grisly. As they homed in, the British ships took carefully timed evasive action, darting one way then another, to avoid the *Bismarck's* powerful guns.

This time luck was with the British, and few of the *Bismarck's* shells found their mark. By 8:59am *King George V* and *Rodney* were both firing steadily. Four salvos a minute were falling around the *Bismarck*, which was now completely obscured by smoke and spray from the huge towering columns of water sent into the air by near misses.

The first and final voyage of the *Bismarck*

At 9:02am a shell from *Rodney* hit *Bismarck* near the bow, and the entire front end of the ship was momentarily swallowed by a blinding sheet of flame. This one shot, ten or so minutes into the battle, was the most crucial of the day. After that, *Bismarck's* two front turrets fired no more. In one, the huge guns pointed down to the deck, in the other, one barrel pointed up, and the other down. In that one explosion, perhaps half the ship's crew had been killed. Only one man from the entire front section survived the battle.

Bismarck may have been the most technologically advanced battleship in the world, but she was completely outgunned. For a further hour, hundreds of shells fell on her. On deck or below, men were blown to pieces or burned to death, as her interior turned into a blazing deathtrap. As the British ships drew closer, *Bismarck's* exceptionally effective construction merely made her destruction even more prolonged. As the shelling continued, fierce fires blazed all over her deck and superstructure, and *Bismarck* began to list to port.

By 10:00am the British ships were close enough to see streams of men leaping into the sea, to save themselves from the flames and still-exploding shells. When it was obvious that the crew were abandoning their ship, Tovey ordered the shelling to stop. Burkard Freiherr von Mullenheim-Rechberg, fire-control officer for the *Bismarck's* after guns, emerged from his battle station and surveyed the damage. "The anti-aircraft guns and searchlights that once surrounded the after station had disappeared without a trace. Where there had been guns, shields, instruments, there was empty space. The superstructure (upper) decks were littered with scrap metal. There were holes in the stack (funnel), but it was still standing..."

Von Mullenheim-Rechberg could see that the ship was slowly capsizing. Amid the carnage and rubble, men were running around, desperately searching for ways to save themselves. Such was the destruction on the decks that not a single lifeboat, life raft or float remained. Amid the smoke and ruin, von Mullenheim-Rechberg saw doctors busy attending to the wounded, giving them pain-killing morphine jabs to ease their agony.

Many men were trapped inside the ship, as fires cut off escape routes, and shells buckled hatches which now no longer opened. Some were able to escape by climbing up shell hoists, wiring shafts or any other kind of duct large enough to take a man. Many others gave up hope and sat where they could, waiting for the ship to go down. But still the *Bismarck* stayed afloat.

During the morning, Tovey was expecting both submarine and air attack by German forces, and was anxious to leave the area as quickly as possible. He ordered any ship with torpedoes left to fire them at the *Bismarck*, to send her to the bottom of the sea. The *Dorsetshire* fired three from close range, and all struck home. Finally, at 10:39am, the *Bismarck* turned over and sank. To this day it is unclear whether or not she sank because of these torpedoes, or because her crew deliberately flooded her, to keep their ship from falling into British hands.

Men in the water near the bow witnessed one final extraordinary scene. Although Lütjens had been killed by shellfire early in the battle, Captain Lindemann had survived. Now he was sighted with a junior officer, standing near the front of the ship, with seawater fast approaching its sinking bows. From his gestures he appeared to be urging this man to save himself. But the man refused and stayed next to Lindemann. Then, as the deck slowly turned over into the sea, Lindemann stopped and raised his hand to his cap in a final salute, then disappeared. Afterwards, one survivor recalled: "I always thought such things happened only in books, but I saw it with my own eyes."

By now the *Dorsetshire* and the destroyer *Maori* were the only remaining ships at the scene. Close to where the *Bismarck* had gone down, British sailors could see hundreds of tiny heads floating in the water. *Bismarck*'s crew had been told that the British shot their prisoners – a sly piece of Nazi propaganda designed to ensure German military forces would always be reluctant to surrender. But as the freezing survivors swam toward the British ships, they discovered this was not the case. Men were hurriedly bundled aboard. But in a cruel twist of fate, a lookout from the *Dorsetshire* spotted a whiff of smoke a couple of miles away which was thought to be a German U-Boat. The British ships were immediately ordered to move off. Although over a hundred men were rescued, 300 were left in the water. As the day wore on, these exhausted men who had seen their hopes of survival raised then crushed, slowly succumbed to the intense cold of the ocean. Only five lived to tell the tale. Three were picked up by a U-boat, and two by a German weather ship. When other German ships arrived on the scene they found only rubble, lifebelts and a few floating bodies.

Bismarck turned completely upside down on her descent to the ocean floor 5km (3 miles) below, and her four huge gun turrets fell from their housings. By the time she hit the slopes of a vast underwater volcano 20 minutes later, she had righted herself, and set off a huge landslide which carried her further down the slope. There she lies today, where she was recently discovered by the marine archaeologist Robert Ballard. In 1989, his underwater cameras showed that the hull remains intact. Shells, barnacles and sundry other small sea creatures line the wooden planks of the deck. And as the fresh paint applied a few days before she sank gradually dissolved in the seawater, the swastikas on *Bismarck*'s bow and stern have made a sinister reappearance.

Cracking Enigma

Germany's secret code, 1941-1945

Kapitänleutnant Fritz-Julius Lemp peered through the periscope of submarine *U-110*. It was late in the morning of May 9, 1941, the last day of his life. Through the narrow lens, which surfaced just above the choppy sea south of Iceland, he could see a convoy of British ships bound for Nova Scotia.

Lemp's wartime service with the German submarine fleet was brief and glorious. In 10 wartime patrols he had sunk 20 ships and damaged another four. Less than a year into the war, and all before he turned 27, he had been presented with the *Iron Cross* 1st and 2nd class, and the *Knight's Cross* – among the most prestigious awards available to German military men. This allowed him to be astonishingly insolent with his senior commanders. One instruction from navy headquarters sent to him on his U-boat received a curt two word dismissal: "S★★★. Lemp".

The medals, and the tolerance which greeted his outbursts, were a recognition of his calling. It was a wonder anyone, on any side of the war, volunteered to serve on submarines. It was an uncomfortable and highly dangerous life. But the reason they did volunteer was that submarines were devastatingly effective. In the course of the war, German U-boats sank 2,603 cargo ships and 175 of their warship escorts. But for such success they paid a terrible price. More than two out of three U-boats were sunk, taking about 26,000 submariners to the bottom of the sea.

U-boats kept in touch with their headquarters via radio signals. Here they would report their own positions and progress, and receive instructions on where to head next. Such reports were sent in code of course. It was a code that had incessantly perplexed the British. Their intelligence service had set up a special code-breaking department at Bletchley Park, Buckinghamshire, to try to crack it. If the British knew where the U-boats were, or where they were going, they could avoid them or hunt them down. For an island so dependent on food and material brought in by cargo ships, cracking the German navy code became one of the most vital tasks of the war.

On that May morning, Lemp was uneasy. He did not usually carry out daytime attacks, especially on convoys protected by warship escorts. It was far more difficult for such escorts to locate his submarine during a night attack. But his fear of losing contact with his quarry overrode such considerations. Just before noon, *U-110* unleashed three torpedoes. Two hit home, sending towering columns of spray into the air by the side of two unlucky ships. But when Lemp ordered a fourth torpedo to be fired, it failed to leave its launch tube.

This minor mishap soon added up to a major disaster for *U-110*. When a torpedo is fired, water is immediately pumped into the forward ballast tanks, to compensate for the missing weight and keep the submarine level under the water. So, even though the torpedo failed to leave its tube, water still poured into the front of the vessel, unbalancing the submarine. Inside *U-110* the crew fought to regain control. During the ensuing disorder, several British warships charged toward the U–boat. Only when Lemp had regained control of his submarine did he check his periscope. Seeing a warship bearing down on him, he immediately decided to dive deeper under the sea – the standard procedure for a submarine under attack. But it was too late. Inside the hull, the crew listened to the dull throbbing of approaching propeller blades. Then came two splashes as a couple of depths charges★ were pitched overboard. With dry mouths and an awful tightness in the pit of their stomachs, the crew of *U-110* waited for the charges to float down toward them.

When the explosions came with a huge thunderous peal, the submarine rocked to and fro as if caught in a hurricane. The main lights went out, and for a few seconds there was a deathly total darkness. Then, blue emergency lighting flickered on. As their eyes adjusted to the dim light, terrified and disoriented men looked over to their captain for

★Heavy canisters loaded with high explosives

reassurance. Lemp had been under attack before, and he played his part to perfection. Leaning his short, stocky frame casually against his periscope mount, hat pushed to the back of his head, he looked like a suburban bus driver plodding though his usual dreary journey. Lemp's act had a serious purpose. If anyone on the submarine panicked and started yelling hysterically, the British ships would pick up the noise on their sound detection equipment, and home in on them rapidly.

Now, a deathly hush settled on the submarine, only disturbed by the occasional ominous creaking, and damage reports from other parts of the boat. Neither depth charge had hit the submarine directly, but the damage they caused was still considerable. The trim controls (which kept the submarine level underwater) had broken and the rudder no longer worked. The batteries had been contaminated with seawater and were now giving off poisonous chlorine gas. The depth gauges gave no reading, so it was impossible to tell whether the submarine was rising or falling in the sea. Worst of all, a steady hissing sound indicated that compressed air containers were leaking. Without this air, the submarine would not be able to blow water out of its ballast tanks and get to the surface. Now, even Lemp could not pretend that everything was going to be OK. "All we can do is wait," he told his men. "I want you all to think of home, or something beautiful."

These soothing words cannot have been much

comfort. In the awful silence that followed, perhaps his crew thought of how their girlfriends or families would greet news of their deaths. More likely than not, in his mind's eye, each man imagined the submarine sinking slowly into the dark depths of the ocean. If that section of the sea was deep, steel plates on the hull would creak and groan until a fluttering in the ears told the crew the submarine's air pressure had been disturbed by water pouring inside the ship. Then the boat would be rent apart beneath their feet, and they would be engulfed by a torrent of black icy water. At such a depth, no one aboard had any chance of reaching the surface.

If that section of the sea was shallow, the submarine might simply sink to the bottom. Then, men would have to sit in the strange blue light, or pitch darkness, shivering in the damp cold, as their submarine gradually filled with water. The corrosive smell of chlorine gas would catch in their throats, and they would slowly suffocate in the foul-smelling air.

But just as the men were convinced they were going to die, *U-110* began to rock gently to and fro. A huge wave of relief swept through the men. This was a motion the crew all recognized – their submarine was bobbing on the surface. Lemp, still playing his bus driver part, announced, "Last stop! Everyone out!" In a well-rehearsed drill, the crew headed for their exit hatches and poured out on to the deck.

But their troubles were not yet over. As they filled

their lungs with fresh sea air, three warships were fast bearing down on them, intending to ram the submarine before it could do more damage. Shells and bullets were whizzing past their ears. But none of the men had any intention of manning the guns on the deck of the *U-110*, or firing any more torpedoes. They had just stared death in the face, and were desperate to abandon their boat.

Men jumped overboard and drowned, others were killed by the shells and bullets that rained down on them. Amid the wild confusion, one of the ship's radio operators found Lemp and asked him whether he should destroy the ship's code books and coding machinery. Lemp shook his head, and gestured impatiently, "The ship's sinking." Below deck, the last few left aboard opened valves to flood their submarine, to make sure it really did sink. Then they too jumped into the frothy, freezing sea.

Aboard *HMS Bulldog*, steaming in to ram the *U-110*, its captain Commander Joe Baker-Cresswell had a sudden change of heart. When he could see that the members of the enemy crew were throwing themselves off their vessel, he ordered his ship to reverse its engines and it slowly came to a halt.

Other British ships, now certain that the *U-110* was no longer a threat, stopped firing. Then, the destroyer *Aubretia* pulled up nearby to rescue the crew. It had been her depth charges that had done so much damage. As Lemp and a fellow officer struggled to stay afloat, they noticed to their horror that the submarine was not going to sink after all. Clearly something had stopped the water from pouring in. Lemp shouted over that they should try to climb back on board to sink their boat. But, just then, a vast, rolling wave swept over them, and the U-boat was carried out of reach. The crew had missed their chance. Most of the men survived in the water long enough to be picked up. Lemp was not one of them.

From the bridge of *HMS Bulldog*, Baker-Cresswell surveyed the submarine with great interest. It was floating low in the water, but did not look as if it would sink immediately. Its crew had either been killed or were being rescued. It seemed likely to have been abandoned. So Baker-Cresswell decided to send in a small boarding party to investigate. This unenviable job went to 20-year-old sub-lieutenant David Balme. Together with eight volunteers, Balme clambered aboard a small boat, lowered from the *Bulldog*, and set off across the choppy sea. As they lurched closer to the *U-110*'s black hull, Balme grew increasingly tense. As the most senior officer in the boarding party, it was his responsibility to lead his men into the submarine. The only way in was through a hatch in the conning tower. There could be submariners inside, waiting to shoot anyone who entered. Even if no one was still on board, it was standard practice on an abandoned submarine to set off explosives on a timed fuse, or flood the boat, to prevent it from falling into enemy hands. Besides, if the crew had completely abandoned it, it was probably taking in water fast, and could sink at any moment.

So, expecting to die from either a bullet or an explosion, or in a torrent of water, Balme lurched off his boat and onto the slippery deck of the *U-110*. His men followed immediately after, but no sooner had the last man clambered aboard than a wave picked up their boat and smashed it into pieces on the deck of the submarine. This was not a good omen.

With his heart in his mouth, Balme climbed the conning tower to find an open hatch at the top. It stood before him, the gateway to his doom. Balme fought back his fears and told himself sternly: "Stop thinking... just do it." He took his pistol from its holster and peered gingerly down into the darkened interior. Immediately, a gust of warm air wafted up to meet him. It contrasted strangely with the icy Icelandic wind blowing off the sea, and would have been inviting had it not smelled so foul. All submarines have a distinct stench. Those not used to it find it almost unbearable. It is the stale dishcloth, rotten cabbage smell of 30 or more men confined for weeks on end in an enclosed, airless environment, unable to bathe properly or clean their clothes.

Balme sensed the impatience of the men behind him. They wouldn't be the first to be shot, but they were just as vulnerable as he was to explosives or a sinking submarine. "Just do it," chided a voice in his head. He swung down into the interior, expecting a bullet right through the buttocks. His boots clanged down the long steel ladder, but there was no one there to greet him. He reached the strange blue interior of the control room, and the others briskly followed. As their eyes grew used to the dim light, they blundered through the vessel, searching for any remaining crew.

But *U-110* was completely deserted. Quickly Balme's party began to search the boat for documents, knowing it could still sink or explode at any moment. Their courage was richly rewarded. Inside the radio operator's cabin was a sealed envelope containing codes and other useful documents, such as signal logs, code instruction procedures, and further code books. But there was also a curious machine that looked like a strange sort of typewriter. It had a keyboard, and one of the men pressed a letter on it. A light on a panel above the keyboard flickered on. The thing was still plugged in! It immediately dawned on Balme that it was a coding machine. Four screws held it to the side of the cabin. These were quickly removed, and the device was carefully put to one side.

It became clear to Balme there must have been complete panic among the crew, to have left everything behind like this. As his search party worked on, the overpowering dread they first felt on entering the boat faded a little. An explosion never came, and neither did the bows of the ship suddenly lurch into the air, throwing them higgledy-piggledy down through the deck sections, just before the *U-110* slipped below the waves. But there were other things to worry about. The *Bulldog*, and other warships guarding the convoy, had gone off to chase other submarines. If the *U-110* sank in the meantime, they had no boat, and no immediate chance of rescue.

Finally, *Bulldog* returned to wait for the boarding party to finish their work. Shortly afterwards, Balme was sitting in the U-boat captain's cramped cabin. While he ate a sandwich which Baker-Cresswell had thoughtfully sent over, he reflected that life was looking up. When his men had finished their search, a boat was sent to collect them, then a tow rope was attached to *U-110*. The following morning, in rough seas, the submarine finally sank. Baker-Cresswell was distraught. A captured submarine was quite a prize, and could even have been manned by a British crew and used again. But he needn't have worried.

News that *HMS Bulldog* had captured a coding machine from the *U-110* caused a sensation at the Admiralty - British naval headquarters. Signals were quickly sent out ordering Baker-Cresswell and his crew to maintain the strictest secrecy. When *Bulldog* reached the navy base of Scapa Flow in Scotland, two naval intelligence officers immediately came on board, eager to examine the items Balme's party had seized. What especially thrilled them was the code machine. "We've waited the whole war for one of these," said one. The documents also excited great interest. The next day, as the *Bulldog* sailed back to its Icelandic patrol, Baker-Cresswell received a thinly veiled message from Dudley Pound, the commander of the Royal Navy. "Hearty Congratulations. The petals of your flower are of rare beauty."

The typewriter-like device Balme's party had found was a fully-working Enigma machine – the ingenious coding instrument devised by the German military. Enigma was used for "scrambling" a message so that it became diabolically difficult to crack. And there were literally billions of possible combinations for each coded message.

Enigma had a keyboard layout similar to a typewriter, but it only contained the 26 letters of the alphabet. When a letter key was pressed, it sent a signal to a plugboard at the front of the machine. This was also arranged in a standard keyboard layout, with a variable arrangement of cable leads which could go from any direction – say from C to T, and then U to K. This was the first stage in the scrambling of a message.

From the plugboard the signal was then routed to a series of replaceable, interconnected rotating wheels, each with all 26 letters of the alphabet around the rim. These scrambled the original letter still further. There were between three and five of these wheels inside the Enigma, depending on the model. The wheels were chosen from a standard selection of eight.

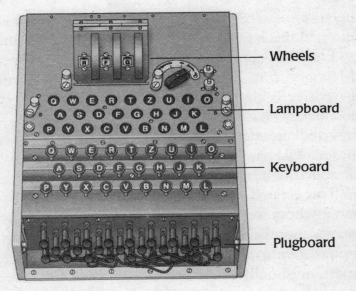

An Enigma machine from 1941

From the wheels the signal was sent to a "lampboard" positioned behind the keyboard, lighting up another letter which the operator would write down. In this way, messages would be fed through for coding, and then transmitted via Morse code as ordinary radio signals.

Enigma, invented in 1919 by German engineer Arthur Scherbius, was a remarkable machine. Each keystroke, even of the same key, produced a different letter. If the operator pressed three Ps, for example, the rotating wheels could produce three different letters – K, J and F, for example. Even on machines with three wheels, it would not begin to produce the same sequence for the same letter until the key had been pressed 16,900 times. This was when the internal mechanism returned to its original position.

Enigma's complexity created its own problems. Messages from one machine to another could only be correctly decoded if both machines were set up identically. Each wheel, for example, had to be inserted in one specific position, and in a specific order. Likewise, the front plugboard had to be arranged in exactly the same way.

This created a particular difficulty for the German navy, whose ships and submarines would be away at sea for months on end. They were sent out with code books giving precise details for how their Enigma machine should be set up for each day of the weeks and months ahead, and which settings should be changed at midnight. It was, of course, essential that such codebooks or coding machines should never fall into enemy hands.

The machine captured by Balme, and all the accompanying material, was sent at once to Bletchley Park. This grand mansion and its grounds had been set up as British intelligence's code-breaking headquarters in 1939, just before the start of the war. Most of the work was done in a makeshift collection of prefabricated huts, with trestle tables and collapsible chairs. It was staffed by some of the greatest mathematical brains in the country. Chief among them was Alan Turing, a Cambridge and Princeton University professor. His ground-breaking work into decoding Enigma messages, using primitive computers, led directly to the kind of computers we all use today.

Turing's team had a gargantuan task. The Enigma code was complex enough to begin with. But to make it even more difficult, the code was changed every day, and coding procedures were regularly updated. In the course of the war, the Enigma machines themselves also went through several design improvements. On top of all this, at the height of the conflict 2,000 messages a day, from all branches of the German armed forces, were being sent to Bletchley for decoding.

Even with the brightest brains in the country, the staff of Bletchley Park could not crack the Enigma code without some direct assistance. They relied on the kind of lucky breaks David Balme's boarding party brought them. These came in dribs and drabs throughout the war. Balme's Enigma machine was not the first to fall into British hands, but it was certainly the most up-to-date. The books and documents he rescued were especially useful. They gave information on settings and procedures for encoding the most sensitive, top-secret information, which the Germans called *Offizier* codes.

Enigma was like a huge jigsaw puzzle. Any codebooks or machines that were captured helped to put the puzzle together for a few days or weeks, until the codes and machines changed. Then, instead of decoding sensitive and highly useful messages about

U-boat positions or air force strikes, code breakers would find themselves churning out reams of meaningless gobbledygook. For the staff at Bletchley Park, such moments provoked heartbreaking disappointment. They were well aware of how their work could save the lives of thousands of people.

In 1997 Balme recalled: "I still wake up at night, fifty-six years later, to find myself going down that ladder." But, thanks to the courage of men like him, the staff of Bletchley Park were provided with vital further opportunities to break their enemy's code.

Death of a salesgirl

Violette Szabo, 1940-1945

It was a strange, sad little ceremony. On May 2, 1950, Tania Szabo, a seven-year-old girl, neatly dressed in her best frock and with a fetching bow in her hair, stood before the ambassador at the French Embassy in London. He crouched down low to kiss her cheek and pinned a medal on her frock – the *Croix de Guerre* – awarded for bravery. Tania was familiar with such ceremonies. She had already met the king, George VI, who had given her a similar award – the *George Cross*. The medals weren't for Tania, of course. They were for her mother, Violette. As the ambassador knelt down, he noticed how strikingly like her mother Tania was. The little girl, once described as looking like "the prettiest doll in the shop", had huge eyes and thick dark hair.

Violette, and Tania's father Etienne, had both died in the war. He had been killed in North Africa shortly after she was born, and had never met her. Violette had died in Germany when Tania was two and a half. Violette, the actual, real Violette, who had cuddled and comforted her, was a fading memory to Tania now. Only fragments and random recollections

49

- the sound of her voice, the dark scent of her perfume - were left. Now Tania remembered her mother mostly from photographs, and her grandparents' stories. And what they told her was that her mother was a hero...

Violette Szabo was a British agent, sent to occupied France to fight against the Nazis. She worked for the SOE (Special Operations Executive), a secret service branch of the armed forces. One of Violette's contemporaries, Odette Sanson, once described her as "the bravest of us all". She was a fine example of how the circumstances and fortunes of war can transform ordinary people into extraordinary heroes.

But perhaps Violette Szabo, a teenager working behind a perfume counter in a Brixton department store when war broke out, was never *that* ordinary. Many of the SOE agents were women who stood out in a crowd. Virginia Hall, was a towering, formidable American who had a wooden leg. Christina Granville was a willowy Pole with the face and figure of a catwalk supermodel. They were hardly the sort of people you wouldn't notice, and neither was Violette. Small - petite - and full of high spirits, one of her senior officers described her wistfully: "She was really beautiful, dark-haired and olive-skinned, with a kind of porcelain clarity..."

She was born Violette Bushell in 1921, to a French mother and English father. Her father set up his own taxi business in Britain and France, and Violette divided her life between both countries. Although the family home was in London, she grew up fluent in both languages, and comfortable with both cultures. Her father, who had met her mother in France during the First World War, was an excellent shot. He regularly horrified his family and friends by shooting apples off Violette's head. As the eldest daughter, Violette took to responsibility easily enough, helping her mother look after her three younger brothers and making herself useful around the house. Seeming much older than her actual age, she once took off to France after a family argument without even telling her parents. She seemed to have inherited her father's talent for shooting too – so much so that local fairgrounds banned her from their shooting galleries because she won too many prizes.

Bright and capable she may have been, but she was not especially academic. She left school at 14 to work as a hairdresser's assistant and then as a shop girl at Woolworths. When war broke out in 1939, Violette gave no thought to joining the armed services. But when France fell to the Nazis in 1940, London was flooded with French soldiers. Violette's mother thought it would be nice to invite one of them home, "to give them a proper French meal" – especially on Bastille Day, July 14, a French national day of celebration. Violette was sent off to a military parade to find a Frenchman to invite. She duly returned with a handsome Foreign Legion officer named Etienne Szabo, whose bravery had already won him several medals. The Bushell family liked Etienne immensely, and within six weeks he and Violette had married.

Barely days after the ceremony, Etienne left England to fight in Abyssinia (now Ethiopia). Violette too decided to "do her bit" – as people said in those days. She joined the Auxiliary Territorial Service (ATS) – a branch of the army where women could do everything male soldiers were expected to do, except front line combat. Violette was assigned to an anti-aircraft battery, where she was well-liked and did whatever she was asked with great enthusiasm.

Etienne returned for a fleeting visit over a year later, in October 1941. During this time, Violette became pregnant, and had to leave the ATS. Tania was born in June 1942. Etienne heard about the safe arrival of his daughter while fighting the German army in North Africa. But, during this intense period of the war, he could not be spared for leave. He was killed at the Battle of El Alamein four months later.

News of his death filled Violette with an intense desire for vengeance. Soon after, out of the blue, she received an official army letter from a "Mr. Potter", asking her to come to an interview at a hotel in central London. Although she did not yet know it, Violette had been contacted by the Special Operations Executive. The SOE had been set up with the intention of organizing opposition to the Nazis, especially in the territories they had conquered. Agents would be dropped by aircraft to rendezvous with local underground fighters, known as "the Resistance". Factories, railway stations and military bases would be bombed. Troops would be ambushed, collaborators assassinated. Where possible, their job was also to stir up civil unrest against the Germans.

The SOE was a secret organization of course, so they could hardly place advertisements in newspapers asking for volunteers. Instead, they recruited more obliquely. Violette's army file noted that she was half-French and bilingual in English and French – qualities which would make her a useful agent.

At the hotel, Violette was directed into a bare room with two chairs and a table. Sitting across from her was "Mr. Potter" – who was actually Major Selwyn Jepson, a recruitment officer for the SOE. He spoke to her mostly in French, explaining that he was looking for people to do "dangerous work" in France. Violette leapt at the chance so readily, Jepson was instantly wary. Impulsiveness was a character trait most unsuited to spying. He asked her to return in a week, to discuss the matter further.

When they met again Jepson did not mince his words. There was a one in four chance that she would be killed, he said. Violette was unperturbed by this, but did make detailed inquiries about her army pension, and financial support for her daughter should she die. At this meeting, Jepson's doubts about her receded. Her enthusiasm, he decided, was genuine, and driven by a desire to avenge her husband's death.

So Violette was recruited, and began to train intensively for her role. Although women were not expected to take part in front line combat, the military made an exception with SOE agents. First she was sent for a three week fitness course to toughen her up. She had always been good at sports, and cycled a lot as a teenager, so she was in good shape already. Then she went up to Scotland to learn how to fight – how to fire a machine gun, kill a guard silently and with her bare hands, destroy bridges and railway lines with explosives, lay an ambush, storm a house – all of which were not considered very ladylike pursuits, especially in the 1940s.

The final part of her training was the most secret of all. She was taught how the Nazis controlled their conquered populations with a mixture of intimidation and cooperation with collaborators. She learned how to assume the identity of another person – whatever alias she would be given on her mission – and how to parachute from an aircraft without breaking a leg. Despite the odd mishap, such as a bad sprain in parachute training, Violette proved a natural in all these activities. But she did struggle with her codes – essential for agents to transmit details of their activities home in secret. Her training complete, Violette was flown to France on her first mission. It was to be a particularly dangerous and difficult one. The German *Gestapo* (secret police) had made many arrests around Rouen, of a group of local Resistance members codenamed the "Salesman" circuit. Violette's job was to assess the strength of those who had evaded capture. Dealing with the French Resistance was never easy. They were divided among themselves, between supporters of the Free French movement in London, and those who were communist. They were also infiltrated by German spies. In the wake of the *Gestapo* arrests, Violette would be arriving in an atmosphere fraught with fear and suspicion.

In April 1944, she was flown to France in a tiny *Lysander* aircraft, which could land and take off in a very small area. Flown over at the same time was a French SOE agent named Philippe Liewer, who had been a journalist before the war. They were dropped off in the countryside around Azay-le-Rideau, where they were met by a small party of Resistance fighters. Quickly hurried off to a safe house for the rest of the night, they went on to Paris the next day. Here Violette took a train to Rouen, to begin her mission. The journey itself was fraught, and full of opportunities for mistakes. German soldiers seemed to flock to Violette. She spent the whole trip refusing offers of assistance, of having her bag carried, of cigarettes... Violette fended off her admirers with a weary shrug – the way she thought a real French woman would act. She did not even want to speak to these soldiers – although her fluency in French was impeccable, she had the trace of an English accent.

Death of a salesgirl

Perhaps the Germans would not have grasped her accent was imperfect, but the French anti-resistance militia, the *Milice*, who collaborated with the Germans, would not be fooled.

For three weeks she snooped around Rouen, trying to find out what had happened to the Resistance group there. She even visited the houses of known Resistance members. Not only did she have to remain undiscovered by the authorities, she had to convince those she came into contact with that she was a genuine British agent – not a spy sent by the Germans, or *Milice*, to winkle out more suspects. Violette had been thrown in at the deep end with a task requiring great tact and courage. Twice she was stopped by police, questioned, and released. She always remained calm, offering a convincing alias, and plausible reasons for being in Rouen. Neither did she let these narrow brushes with disaster deter her. She carried out her work with great skill, and established beyond doubt that the Salesman circuit had been well and truly broken.

Violette enjoyed being back in France – even under these dreadful circumstances. When her work in Rouen was finished, she took a train back to Paris where she had arranged to meet up with Philippe Liewer. From there they would go south to the countryside outside Chateauroux to be picked up by another *Lysander*. Violette had two days to herself in Paris. She roamed the streets, which she knew well from her youth, although wartime Paris was much drabber than the bustling city it once was. But there were still items to be had in the shops that could not be found in England. Violette picked up some perfume for herself and her mother. She also bought a beautiful dress for Tania, and some chic Parisian clothes for herself – three dresses and a sweater. Minor alterations were made to the fit, and Violette went to collect them on the morning she was due to return to England. After a final quick flit around the shops, she left.

On the night of April 30 she waited anxiously with Liewer for their planes to arrive – which could have been any time from 10:30pm to 1:30 the next morning. Each was to travel separately in a *Lysander*, with other French agents who were also being picked up. This arrangement tacitly acknowledged the danger of the flight back. If one plane was shot down and all aboard were killed, then at least the other would carry one agent who could tell the Special Operations Executive what had happened to the Salesman circuit. It was a well-justified fear. The pilot of Liewer's plane was killed on his next mission.

The pick up was uneventful and Violette felt a surge of relief as the plane lurched off its bumpy runway to vanish into the dark. But outside Chateaudun the *Lysander* flew close to a German airfield. Immediately the sky was filled with searchlights, and anti-aircraft shells burst around the plane. Violette was terrified, and with good reason.

The Lysander might have been able to land and take off on a matchbox, but it was a slow, lumbering aircraft, and was an easy target both for gunners on the ground and night fighter aircraft. The pilot twisted, turned, dived and banked to get away from the lights, and Violette was thrown violently around the aircraft cabin. But luck was with them and, as the plane flew on, the shell bursts grew fewer and more distant.

When they arrived at the RAF airfield of Tempsford, disaster struck again. The plane had had such a narrow escape over Chateaudun that the rubber on one of its wheels had been ripped to shreds. The landing was a near disaster. Violette was so disoriented she imagined they had crashed in France. When the pilot came to help her out of the plane she mistook him for a German come to arrest her. He was greeted with a bewildering tirade of angry French, but when Violette realized she was back in England, she flung her arms around him and gave him a kiss.

Now it was late spring, and an invasion of France from England was imminent. When the invasion came, Allied troops would land on the beaches of Normandy. It was also hoped that the French Resistance would rise up behind German lines to help them. Before and during the invasion, members of the SOE were dropped in France to organize such an uprising, and Violette was among them.

The invasion began at first light on June 6, 1944. The following night, Violette boarded a *B-24 Liberator* bomber at Tempsford, with Philippe Liewer and two other French agents. Whatever private fears they had about the parachute jump to come, and the mission ahead, they kept to themselves. The crew remember their four agents passing the time on the flight out by playing cards together. Before she jumped, Violette staggered around the lurching plane to kiss each member of the crew. When the *B-24* flew over the "drop zone" - the area where Resistance members had agreed to meet them - lights were lit on the ground to let the pilot know they were waiting. Then, with a wink to her fellow agents, Violette jumped just after 1:30am. She landed safely and right on target - outside the village of Sussac close to the town of Limoges.

Supplies for the Resistance, and the agents' personal possessions, were dropped in separate packages, and then hurriedly gathered up and bundled into waiting cars. All four agents were taken to a grocer's shop in Sussac and given a meal and a bed for the night. Violette felt exhausted - she had been up almost all night - but huge relief too. An agent dropping into France at night never really knew who would be waiting for them. Sometimes they would be betrayed, or messages would be intercepted, and German soldiers would be there to meet them.

For this mission, Philippe Liewer had been

charged with the difficult job of directing Resistance forces around Limoges. Violette was there to help him. They had been briefed to expect a well-organized and professional team of fighting men and women. But the reality was very different. There were around 800 Resistance members under Liewer's command, but they were untrained, with no experience of fighting, and led by what he described as "the most incapable people I have ever met." Liewer found that different groups in the area refused to cooperate with each other. Also, they seemed very reluctant to engage their enemy. Not one of the targets they had been asked to strike before the agents arrived had been attacked. When Liewer tried to organize any attacks, he had to spend hours arguing his case to local commanders.

Barely a couple of days into his mission, Liewer lost patience with the men he had been sent to command. But he had other options. There were Resistance groups in nearby areas, and he made steps to contact them. Violette was ordered to meet up with a Jacques Poirier, the leader of a group about 160km (100 miles) to the south. So on the morning of June 10 she and another Resistance fighter named Jacques Dufour set off in a large black Citröen. The plan was for Dufour to take her halfway, and then for Violette to cycle the remaining distance. If they were stopped and questioned, either by German soldiers, or the *Milice*, they agreed to say that Violette was an antique dealer visiting one of her shops in the south.

A bicycle was strapped to the roof of the car, but Violette also insisted on taking a couple of Sten guns – small, light machine guns. Why they took the guns will forever remain a mystery. The likelihood of being stopped and searched was high, and there was no convincing reason why an antique dealer and her driver would be carrying these British combat weapons.

On the way down south, they picked up another Resistance member named Jean Bariaud, who would keep Dufour company on his way back to Sussac. Not long after they picked up Bariaud, at around ten o'clock that morning, they drove through the village of Salon-la-Tour. Straight ahead of them was a German roadblock. Soldiers immediately ordered the car to stop. They were bound to be searched. Dufour waved back in a friendly manner as he neared the roadblock, but 30m (33 yards) from the block he stopped the car suddenly and all three passengers jumped out. According to eyewitness reports, Bariaud, who was unarmed, ran up the road, but Dufour and Violette started firing at the soldiers with their Sten guns. Using the car as cover, Dufour kept up steady small bursts of fire, and shouted over to Violette to head for a wheat field next to the road, and then to some woods which were a few hundred yards away. Under heavy fire, Violette dashed into the wheat, and then began firing too, so Dufour could follow.

Death of a salesgirl

The wheat field may have been thick, but it was easy enough for the soldiers to track the position of their fleeing foes. Military vehicles raced up to the field, and machine gun fire raked the wheat. Soldiers soon surrounded the field, and whenever they saw wheat stalks twitching they would aim a withering burst of fire. Dufour and Violette made exhaustingly slow progress - fearing that every movement would bring a hail of bullets, but they edged slowly toward the woods. They fought well, both firing off occasional short blasts, to keep the soldiers from charging into the field after them.

By now Violette was exhausted. Her clothes were badly ripped, and she was covered with scratches. She told Dufour she did not have the strength to run through the woods, but she would cover his escape, firing toward the German soldiers as he crawled into the wood. She knew she would either die in the coming fight, or be shot as a spy soon after it, and she was sacrificing her own life for her comrade. Dufour could see she was in no mood to argue. He escaped from the field, and found a perfect hiding place - a haystack next to a nearby farm.

Here Dufour lay, still and silent. After half an hour German troops arrived, and with them was Violette Szabo. Peering though the hay, he noticed she was limping, and had probably sprained an ankle in the chase. Dufour could hear them angrily questioning her about him. She laughed and told them: "You can run after him. He is far away by now." As she sat nearby, smoking a cigarette, the officer in charge of the soldiers told her she was the bravest woman he had ever met, and saluted as she was taken away.

The following day, Violette was driven to Limoges and, from there, to Fresnes prison on the outskirts of Paris. From here she was regularly taken for interrogation, to *Gestapo* headquarters at 84 avenue Foch in the middle of the city. Although she was questioned aggressively, and treated harshly, she was not tortured. Strangely, the *Gestapo* did not usually torture British agents, but were merciless with the French.

By early August 1944, the *Gestapo* decided they were not going to learn anything useful from Violette Szabo. On August 8 she left Paris for the last time, along with two other SOE agents, Denise Bloch and Lilian Rolfe. Their destination was the notorious Ravensbrück concentration camp for women, in northern Germany. The three SOE women were taken to the Paris Gare de l'Est station, where they were joined by several other captured British agents and put on a train under heavy guard. The men were taken to a special prison carriage and the women were chained together and sat in ordinary compartments with an armed escort. The train moved to the German border so slowly they were still in France the following afternoon. Just after 2:00pm they were attacked by Allied planes. Although many on board fled as soon as the attack began, including the German guards, the prisoners were left chained together or locked in their carriages. As bullets buzzed around their heads, and bombs exploded nearby, Violette and another woman crawled through the train corridors with water for the men in the prison carriage, who had not been given anything to drink for several hours. When the planes flew off, the guards returned, and the journey continued.

Ravensbrück was not a death camp, like Auschwitz or Treblinka, but it was almost as grim. Although some prisoners were executed there, most were sent to Ravensbrück to work, but harsh conditions meant many died. Originally built to house 6,000 women prisoners, it was enlarged during the war to take 24,000. When Violette arrived, there were 80,000, crammed behind its barbed wire and electric fences.

Here the day began at 3:00 every morning, when prisoners were roused by a siren from their lice-ridden straw bedding, where they slept two to a bunk. Roll call was at 3:45am and prisoners had to stand for hours to be counted, in all weathers and seasons, dressed only in their thin prison clothes. Then, names were called for work parties, and they were marched off for the day.

By the time Violette reached Ravensbrück, she had grown painfully thin, but her spirit was far from crushed. She met other captured Resistance workers and immediately began to make plans to escape. But before long, Violette and 500 other women were transferred to another camp, named Torgau, on the River Elbe. They were set to work in a munitions factory. Here too she planned an escape, and got as far as obtaining a key for one of the camp gates. But a woman Violette did not know well found out. She was not trusted by her fellow prisoners, so Violette threw the key away before it was discovered.

Conditions at Torgau were much better than at Ravensbrück, but some of the women objected to working in an arms factory, producing shells and bullets for the Nazis. They refused to work. It was a brave but pointless stand. Fritz Sühren, the camp commandant at Ravensbrück, was called in to deal with the mutiny. Half the women were sent to another factory, and half, including Violette, were sent to a camp at Königsberg in East Prussia. Here, as autumn turned to winter, they were set to work in the fields and forests, clearing trees and vegetation from ground that had frozen hard. Not only did they have to wear the thin summer clothes they had arrived in – Violette had a blue silk frock with short sleeves – they were fed an inadequate diet of soup made of water and unwashed potato peelings.

This was treatment designed to break the spirit of even the hardiest soul, and Violette grew increasingly depressed. But, even here, prisoners found comfort in friendship. When Violette returned from the fields, frozen to the bone and in deep despair, one of her friends at the camp, Marie Lecomte, would hug her to warm her up, and give her food she had saved from her own paltry ration. In the depths of winter, as further punishment, the women were refused fuel for their hut heater. As December wore on, Violette and her fellow prisoners grew increasingly skeletal. Many of the women on work parties dropped down dead, from exhaustion and cold.

In early 1945, the authorities at Königsberg received orders to transfer Violette back to Ravensbrück. This was not good news. When she found out, Violette went at once to her friend Marie and sobbed in her arms. Certain she would be killed, Violette wrote her family's address on a sheet of paper, and gave it to Marie. Then the two women made a pact: if either of them died, the other would look after their family. Just before Violette left, she kissed Marie seven times – one kiss for each member of the family she had left behind. She asked Marie to travel to London to tell them what had happened to her, and kiss them all from her.

Violette left Königsberg at 5:00 one morning, along with the two SOE agents who had been with her on the train from Paris – Denise Bloch and Lilian Rolfe. For some reason, the three women were given new clothing, and soap and a comb. Now Violette had a blouse, a skirt and a coat to fend off the cold, instead of her thin summer dress.

They arrived back in Ravensbrück to be placed immediately in solitary confinement. It was obvious that something was going to happen. Alone in her cell, Violette must have pondered the strange twists of fate that led her to Ravensbrück. If she had not chosen Etienne Szabo on that fateful day back in July 1940, the chain of events that had led her to captivity and imminent execution would never have begun.

The stay in Ravensbrück was brief. The war was coming to its inevitable end and Germany's Nazi elite were determined to extract maximum vengeance before power was wrested away from them. At *Gestapo* headquarters in Berlin, a list of names of British agents due for immediate execution had been drawn up. The list included Violette, Denise and Lilian. A few days after their return, on a bleak February early evening, the sound of marching feet was heard outside their cell doors. The doors clanged open, and each woman was ordered out. They were marched as a group to a block next to the crematorium, close to the inner wall of the camp. Here, waiting for them was camp commandant Fritz Sühren, and a small party of other camp officials including the camp doctor, ready to carry out a grisly ritual.

Sühren read from a document informing the three women they were to be executed. Then, one by one, they were made to kneel down on a step between two camp buildings, and shot. As a method of execution it was, at least, mercifully brief. Denise and Lilian were too weak to stand without help, but Violette, still only 23, walked to her death with great courage. The last thing she saw was a bleak, narrow, dimly lit alley between two buildings, before a single bullet to the back of her neck ended her brief life. Immediately after the executions the three bodies were burned, and all traces of Violette, Denise and Lilian vanished from the face of the Earth.

When peace came to Europe, in the late spring of 1945, Violette's family waited for news of their daughter. They knew that she had been captured by the Germans, but had no inkling of her fate. But as the spring turned to summer, and it slowly became obvious that Violette was not among the survivors of liberated prisoner-of-war and concentration camps, they began to fear the worst. To put an end to the uncertainty, SOE dispatched some of their staff to discover what had happened to their missing agents. Camp officials at Ravensbrück were interrogated, and it was established that Violette Szabo had been executed in February 1945 - a mere three months before the end of the war.

Marie Lecomte, Violette's friend at Königsberg, survived the war. When she tried to get in touch with Violette's family via the British military authorities, she was discouraged from doing so. Perhaps they felt that hearing an account of the last desperate months of Violette's life would be too painful for the family. For years Marie was haunted by her failure. She ran a restaurant at Morlaix, and whenever British people visited, she would ask if they knew Violette's family. Then, in 1958, sorting though some old possessions, she discovered a newspaper cutting about Violette and her family, published a year or so after the war had ended. At the time she was given it, Marie had been extremely ill, and had not realized its significance. The newspaper was contacted, and Marie was put in touch with the Bushell family. She visited them, and was finally able to kiss each one, just as she had promised.

Stalin's female "Falcons"

Russia's women pilots, 1941-1945

Operation Barbarossa, the Nazi attack on Soviet Russia in June 1941, was the biggest invasion in the history of the world. Over three and a half million soldiers, with 4,000 tanks, and 5,000 aircraft, poured over the frontier. Their aim: to reach the Soviet capital Moscow by the time the winter arrived. And they almost did it too. Over 4,000 of the flimsy, obsolete planes of the Russian air force were destroyed in the first week of fighting. During the autumn, nearly 20,000 Russians were dying every day in their struggle to repel the Nazi invaders. By October 1941, advanced units of some German divisions were so close to Moscow they could see sunlight glinting on the Kremlin's golden domes.

Hitler was supremely confident of victory. "We have only to kick in the door and the whole rotten structure will come tumbling down," he said before the campaign began. Nazi armed forces were expected to overrun the country in six to ten weeks. To begin with, Russia's fighting forces were poorly equipped and poorly led, but they resisted the invasion with exceptional courage and tenacity. "The

Russians fight with a truly stupid fanaticism," Hitler fretted. He had good reason to. The invasion would turn out to be the greatest mistake he ever made.

Among those fighting against the Nazi invaders were thousands of women – the Soviets had the only fighting forces that allowed women in combat. This is the story of a small group of women who flew combat missions with the Russian air force...

As Soviet losses mounted during *Operation Barbarossa*, Marina Raskova, Russia's most famous woman pilot, met with Soviet dictator Joseph Stalin. She argued that Russian women could make up the huge losses suffered by Soviet air force pilots. Stalin was not sympathetic to ideas of female equality, but these were desperate times. He agreed. Shortly after, Raskova broadcast on nationwide Soviet radio. She appealed for women volunteers to join three new fighter and bomber regiments she was forming. These regiments would be staffed entirely by women – from pilots to ground crew, such as mechanics and weapons specialists. Soviet newspapers, who referred to all fighter pilots as "Stalin's Falcons", picked up on the story too, and gave Raskova's idea great coverage.

Among those listening was Tamara Pamyatnykh (pronounced Pam-yat-nik) from Rostov-on-Don. As a teenager Pamyatnykh had idolized Raskova, who had pioneered flights out to the far east of Russia, making one legendary 26-hour flight across 11 time zones. Russia's communist regime brought great hardship and fear to its citizens, but not everything it did was bad. Pamyatnykh was part of a new generation of Russian women, born just after the 1917 Revolution. For the first time in Russian history, women like her from ordinary backgrounds had been given an education and undreamed of opportunities. Some of Raskova's volunteers, for example, had already learned to fly with Soviet youth organizations.

Pamyatnykh and two friends immediately headed north to the capital to join Raskova's airborne regiments. They arrived in Moscow on October 15 to find the city in turmoil. With Nazi troops fast approaching, stories were sweeping through the city that the government had fled. In fact it wasn't true, but citizens had every right to fear their city would fall. There was panic in the streets, and policemen with loudspeakers had to appeal for calm.

Eventually Pamyatnykh and her friends found the office building of the Aviation Ministry, and volunteered their services. They were sent on a slow train journey to the town of Engels, north of Stalingrad, to learn how to fly. With new pilots needed so desperately, training that would normally take two years was crammed into an exhausting six months. Pamyatnykh and her fellow fliers had to make do with uniforms that were far too big for them. Boots had to be stuffed with newspapers to make them fit. In the 1940s, before powered controls were invented, a pilot needed some physical strength to fly a plane. One bomber the women flew was especially difficult to manage. On take-off, both the pilot and her navigator had to hold down the control stick together to operate the wing flaps that raised the plane into the air.

The aircraft most of the women trained on was a *Polkarpov PO-2*, an old-fashioned biplane made of canvas and wood. It had a top speed of only 130kmph (81mph). Designed in 1927, it looked ridiculously old-fashioned next to the sleek and deadly *Messerschmitt 109s* and *Focke-Wulf 190s* the German fighter pilots flew. German troops contemptuously nicknamed the *PO-2* the "sewing machine", because its small engine sounded just like one. But the *PO-2* had its uses. It may have been slow, but it was very sturdy, and perfect for surprise attacks. At night, Soviet *PO-2* pilots would cut their engines and silently glide over the German front lines, dropping bombs on them by hand.

During the winter of 1942-43, pilot losses in the Russian air force were running at 50% a year – especially around the Don and Volga regions, where fighting was at its heaviest. This was where Tamara Pamyatnykh found herself stationed with the 586th Fighter Regiment. Here, one of her greatest friends was Raisa Surnachevskaya (Sur-na-chev-sky-ah). Both women had moved on from the bumbling *PO-2s* they trained on, to the much faster *Yak* fighter. The *Yak* was still not as good a plane as the German fighters. Yet, like its namesake, the hairy Tibetan cow, it was sturdy, dependable and agile. But like many Russian weapons, it lacked such basic essentials, such as a radio, at a time when this was a standard piece of equipment for German, American and British pilots. In fact, the *Yak* did not even have a fuel gauge. Pilots had to guess, from their knowledge of average flying time on a full tank of fuel, when they needed to land to refuel.

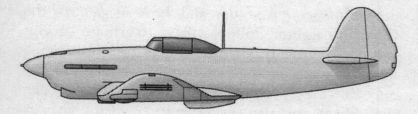

A Soviet air force *Yak* fighter

At the height of the fighting, Pamyatnykh and Surnachevskaya were called on to intercept a single German reconnaissance aircraft over Kastornaya on the Volga. Here the Soviet army was massing its forces to mount a counterattack against the Germans. Meanwhile, the rest of their squadron were sent to guard a bridge which was under threat from air attack. It was March 19, 1943. The epic Battle of Stalingrad, the turning point of the war, had just ended with a Soviet victory, but the Nazis were far from finished.

When the two women reached their position they did not find their single enemy plane. Instead there was a huge formation of 42 *Junkers 88* and *Dornier 217* bombers. They must have felt they had just minutes to live. But, despite being hopelessly outnumbered, they didn't hesitate. Pamyatnykh and Surnachevskaya dived down, with the Sun behind them to blind their enemy, and flew straight into the middle of the bomber pack. In an instant, machine gunners trained their weapons on the Soviet *Yaks*, concentrating their fire above and below, where there was less danger of hitting another German bomber in crossfire. Pamyatnykh darted in and out of the formation, firing steadily whenever a target appeared in front of her, all the while keeping an anxious lookout for any German fighter escorts which might arrive to protect the bombers. One long burst of fire raked the entire cockpit of a *Junkers 88*, and at once its gunners fell silent. The bomber dipped out of formation, beginning a long steep dive which ended a minute later with a fiery explosion. There were no parachutes.

Not that Pamyatnykh was able to watch the plane's final moments. She was frantically weaving to avoid a steady stream of fire from a tight formation of *Dornier 217*s. For an instant one of them loomed in front of her, and Pamyatnykh fired a long burst, watching her bullets burst in tatters of steel and fabric all along the *Dornier*'s wing. As Pamyatnykh veered off sharply to the right, the fuel tanks on the bomber ignited, and the plane exploded. Fragments flew around her and smoke and oil smeared greasy trails across her windscreen.

Thrown around in her seat as her plane cartwheeled across the sky, Pamyatnykh had no time to feel fear: she was in a constant state of unreal, breathless excitement. Above her she saw another bomber diving down, a fierce fire blazing in one engine. Surnachevskaya was finding her targets too. Then Pamyatnykh climbed for another attack. Streams of machine gun fire looped up to meet her and she rolled the *Yak* to and fro to avoid the bullets. She picked out another *Dornier* at the edge of the pack and lined up her plane behind it. But when she pressed the machine gun button on her control stick, nothing happened. The *Yak* had run out of ammunition. In the heat of the moment, Pamyatnykh decided to ram her target. She was so close she could even see the terrified face of the tail gunner and his mousey-grey uniform. But then, just as impact seemed inevitable, the *Yak* spun out of control. As she dropped out of the sky, Pamyatnykh saw that one of her wings had been shot off. Quick as a flash, feeling perfectly calm, she threw back the perspex cockpit cover, and dropped from the plane. Her parachute opened, and Pamyatnykh landed in a field shortly after her *Yak* had nose-dived into the ground.

Only when she had landed did Pamyatnykh notice that her face was covered with blood. How she had been injured was a mystery to her. She looked up at the whirling formations above her. Surnachevskaya was still up there, alone among the formations of bombers. A thick black plume of smoke trailing to the ground told her that her friend had downed another bomber. But her latest victory had cost her dearly. Surnachevskaya's *Yak* had been hit too. Not as badly as Pamyatnykh's, but the engine was backfiring badly, and the controls felt sluggish in her hand. Surnachevskaya knew there was nothing more she could do against the bombers, but she would try, at least, to land her plane so it could be repaired and flown again. This brave decision was far more dangerous than parachuting down and leaving the plane to crash. She coasted down low, close to where Pamyatnykh had landed, and touched down in a flat field.

Meanwhile, Pamyatnykh was still in trouble. A group of angry peasants had surrounded her, and one was aiming a shotgun straight at her. Despite her protestations they were convinced she was a German pilot. They were all set to lynch her, but fortunately a Russian army officer driving by came to help her. On the journey back, as Pamyatnykh removed her heavy leather flying helmet, the driver kept turning around to stare at her in amazement. "Yes, she's a woman," said the officer, trying to sound blasé, while hiding his own astonishment. Pamyatnykh, continually working alongside other women pilots, had forgotten there was anything unusual about it.

Some women proved themselves to be such good combat pilots that they left the women's regiments to fly as "free hunters" in other squadrons. One was Lilya Litvak, the highest scoring woman. ace of the war. Reports vary, but she certainly shot down between 11 and 12 German planes. Described by her comrades as "strikingly pretty", she was so small her feet didn't even reach the foot control pedals of her *Yak*, which had to be specially adjusted. She was fond of flowers, and painted two on either side of her cockpit, earning her the nickname "The White Rose". Whenever she shot down a German plane, she would have a small flower painted on the nose of her *Yak*. She soon became famous as a daredevil pilot and was awarded a *Gold Star Hero of the Soviet Union* medal. Litvak flew missions with her fellow pilot and lover, Alexei Salomaten, until he was shot down and killed. Lilya saw it all happen, and for the rest of her life she carried a photograph of the two of them sitting together on the wing of his plane.

Lilya was never the same after Salomaten died. She flew relentlessly, almost as if she didn't wish to have a minute to herself to grieve. She told her friends that she imagined every German plane she intercepted was the one that had shot down Alexei. At the end of the day she would just collapse exhausted in her bunk. Her friends grew concerned about her. Especially her mechanic, another woman, named Ina Pasportnikova.

During the war pilots on all sides kept a tally of

the aircraft they shot down, in symbols on the side of their planes. On one occasion, shortly after Alexei's death, Lilya was flying a combat mission when she came across a German *Messerschmitt 109*. It had the ace of spades painted on the side, and a whole chart of downed planes displayed on the tail. There were twenty in all. Litvak and the *Messerschmitt* locked on to each other, and chased around the sky in a grim duel. After 15 minutes or so of intense combat, the *Messerschmitt* burst into flames. The pilot bailed out and was captured by Soviet soldiers as soon as he landed.

Litvak flew home to her base, feeling happy for the first time since Salomaten's death. She had had a narrow escape. When she landed she called to Pasportnikova to paint another flower on the *Yak*, which was covered with bullet holes from her day's fighting.

Later that evening, an army truck arrived at her air base. Inside was the German pilot Litvak had just shot down. He was a tall, physically imposing man and, at 40, quite old for a combat pilot. On his chest were rows of medal ribbons. He carried himself with great confidence, perhaps even arrogance, and seemed quite unafraid of his captors. He had been asked if he would like to meet the pilot who shot him down, and had replied that he would be delighted to meet such an accomplished man.

When Litvak was introduced to him, he stood up from his chair and abruptly demanded to be introduced to the real pilot, rather than "this schoolgirl". So Litvak explained, slowly through an interpreter, exactly what had happened in their duel, where it had taken place, and how it had ended. Gradually the German pilot seemed to shrink in size, and slowly sank back in his chair. He was so angry he had been shot down by a woman, he tore the medal ribbons off his chest and threw them across the room in a rage.

After this magnificent personal victory Lilya seemed to be living on borrowed time. One day she was set upon by three fighters and crash-landed in a field. A few days later, her plane caught fire and she had to bail out at very low altitude. Her parachute barely opened before she hit the ground. Eventually it was Lilya's fame that cost her her life. On the late afternoon of August 1, 1943, when she was still only 22, she set off on her fourth mission of that day. (Unlike their allies, Soviet pilots often flew several missions a day. When fighting was at its most intense, they even had to snatch meals in their cockpit, while their plane took on more fuel.) That morning, she had already shot down two aircraft. Litvak was last seen hurling through the sky with eight German fighters on her tail. No doubt they had recognized the white flower on her plane, and were making a determined effort to bring her down. No one saw her die. Her plane, with her body still inside it, was only discovered in 1990. Russia is always immensely proud of its heroes. Almost 50 years after her death, Litvak was given a state funeral attended by the Soviet president, Mikhail Gorbachev.

Despite their successes and undoubted courage, not everyone in the Soviet air force was pleased to see women pilots joining combat squadrons. One woman volunteer recalls being told, "Things may be bad, but we're not so desperate that we're going to put little girls like you up in the sky. Go home and help your mother." Some men refused to fly with the "free hunter" women pilots, or have women as part of their ground crew. It was for these practical reasons Marina Raskova had made her squadrons women only. Some women didn't always behave exactly like their fellow male pilots either. Recently, combat pilot Valentina Petrachenkova told journalist Jonathan Glancey, "The only times I remember being really scared was once when I got into what seemed like an irrecoverable spin... the other (time) was when I flew with a mouse waltzing across the inside of my windscreen. I screamed and screamed! But I wasn't very frightened when I had to climb onto the wing of a parachute plane to drag back in a man who had lost his nerve. I don't know why."

Marina Raskova's three women's regiments flew combat missions right until the end of the war, although she herself was killed in action in 1943, at the age of 31. By the time the war ended in May

1945, 12% of the pilots in the Soviet air force were women. Pamyatnykh and Surnachevskaya both survived the war. Surnachevskaya was four months pregnant when she stopped flying combat missions. At the time of writing, both women are formidable grandmothers, and extremely proud of the role they played in the war.

The book-keeper's storage problem

Adolf Eichmann and the Wannsee Conference 1942

Snow fell soft and silent around the shores of Wannsee, cloaking the forest, parkland and elegant villas around the famous lake. Throughout the morning of January 20, 1942, one of the larger villas received a steady stream of chauffeur–driven cars. Arriving at the villa was a succession of 15 of the most senior members of the Nazi government and its elite SS armed forces. As they entered the marble entrance hall, their coats were swept from their shoulders by fawning functionaries, and their arrival was silently noted. Among them were representatives from the Chancellery, the Race and Resettlement Office, the Ministry of Foreign and Eastern Territories, the Justice Ministry, the *Gestapo*, and the SS. Most had come from nearby Berlin, but some of the army men had been called in from the horror and chaos of the Russian Front, or from other conquered territory in the East. For them, the placid winter scene at Wannsee seemed to belong to some strange parallel universe.

The book-keeper's storage problem

The villa where they assembled, with its marbled staircases and rooms lined with wooden panels, was a substantial three-floored mansion. It had once belonged to a Jewish businessman, but had long since been taken over by the German government. On that January day it was to be the scene of one of the most obscene conferences in human history.

Organizing the preparation of the conference, coordinating the arrival of the delegates, the staff to attend to them, and the buffet prepared for lunch, was Adolf Eichmann. An Austrian Nazi in his late 30s, he was head of the *Gestapo*'s Jewish affairs section. Eichmann was a curiously quiet and rather anonymous man, once memorably described as looking like a book-keeper. He lacked the charisma and spark of some of his more notable colleagues, but he had a reputation for carrying out orders with great thoroughness and efficiency. As the morning progressed, he noted with some satisfaction how well his conference was proceeding.

Last to arrive at Wannsee was Eichmann's boss, SS General Reinhard Heydrich. As head of the Reich Security Main Office, he was one of the most powerful men in Nazi Europe. Tall, blond and handsome, Heydrich was everything Eichmann was not. A former international-level fencer and naval officer, he looked like the epitome of the "Aryan"★ superman – a creature from a Nazi propaganda film. In his most famous photograph, Heydrich stares out

84 ★Aryan was the Nazi term for "pure-blooded" Germans.

with merciless eyes and a cruel mouth. He looks like a stern headmaster about to administer a severe beating to a gaggle of rebellious pupils. No doubt that was the image he wanted to project to the world. In person, the brisk and efficient Heydrich could ooze charm and amiability. But those who crossed him would find themselves subject to chilling threats, made in the casual manner of a Roman emperor, secure in his power of life and death over those around him.

So the conference began. In a haze of cigarette smoke, and the slightly oiled and jovial atmosphere of men who have had a couple of glasses of wine or spirits before lunch, the purpose of the meeting was made plain. Heydrich announced that he had been charged by Hitler's deputy, Hermann Göring, with "the responsibility for working out the final solution of the Jewish problem" in Nazi territory. The various representatives around him were there to ensure the government cooperated effectively with this venture.

Like all supporters of the Nazis, these distinguished and often highly educated men were broadly sympathetic to Hitler's corrosive hatred of the Jews. During the nine years of Nazi rule, heightened and reinforced by a constant barrage of anti-Semitic propaganda, they had grown to think of all Jews with repugnance and fear – perhaps as people today would regard a swarm of diseased rats, or a particularly malignant virus.

Nonetheless, what Heydrich had to report was

utterly monstrous. So much so, that he still felt the need to couch his words to these hard line Nazis in innocuous phrases, to lessen the impact of what he was saying. He explained to the assembled delegates, with statistics gathered directly by Eichmann, that there was a "storage problem" with the eight million or so Jews in German-held territory. Originally, the Nazis had merely intended to expel them, but the war had closed the borders, making this impossible. Heydrich gradually led his delegates around to the view that the only possible option left to Germany, with regard to the Jews, was "evacuation". As the conference went on, it slowly dawned on those assembled around the polished oak table what "evacuation" actually meant. What they were talking about was the cold-blooded murder of eight million people – maybe even eleven million, if Germany succeeded in conquering all of Europe.

Of course, there were a few objections. Even among men like these, the idea of murder on this scale was too horrific to contemplate. But eventually, with the odd silky threat here, and a sharp exhortation there, Heydrich gained the approval of all those assembled. Once this "solution" was accepted, the delegates, with their customary efficiency, decided that it would be economic to house the Jews in concentration camps and put them to work on road and factory building projects, where "natural diminution" (that is, death from exhaustion and illness) would gradually reduce their numbers.

The old, the sick, and children would not be suitable for such projects, so they would be disposed of as soon as possible.

Since the war began, SS troops in Poland and Russia, known as *Einsatzgruppen*, or "action squads", had been systematically shooting Jews in their thousands. But their officers had reported how demoralizing and unpleasant their men had found the job – especially the killing of women and children. So, it was decided the most efficient way to eradicate the Jews that couldn't be used for work, would be gas. In special death camps, hundreds at a time could be herded into gas chambers disguised as shower rooms, to have the life choked out of them quickly and efficiently. Such chambers could dispose of, say, 600 an hour. Working around the clock, they could "evacuate" thousands of Jews a day. Within a year, if all went to plan, Europe would be *Judenfrei*, or "Jew free".

Afterwards, when the delegates had gone, Heydrich, Eichmann, and *Gestapo* chief Heinrich Müller sat down by the fireplace. They smoked a celebratory cigar and drank a toast to a job well done. According to Eichmann, as the drink flowed they began to sing, and arm in arm they danced a jig around the plush chairs and oak tables of the Wannsee villa.

Four months later, Heydrich was mortally wounded in Prague when he was attacked by two Czech soldiers. He died on June 4. In retaliation,

The book-keeper's storage problem

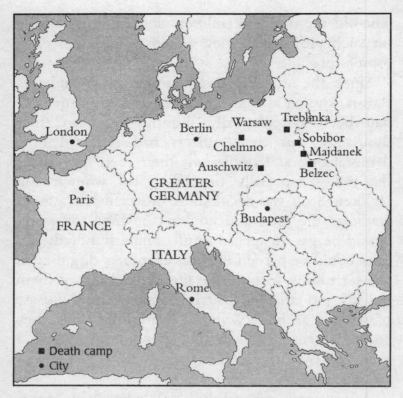

Map of Europe showing the main death camps

German troops murdered nearly 1,500 Czechs, loosely accused of aiding the assassins. Then, for good measure, they also destroyed the Czech village of Lidice, killing all its male inhabitants, and sending its women and children to concentration camps.

By then, the work agreed at Wannsee had begun. From the Gulf of Finland to the Caucasus mountains, from France's Atlantic coast to the island of Crete and the North African shores of Libya, in all areas controlled by the Nazis, Jews were gradually rounded up. Some were shot, or gassed in special vans designed for the process. But most were placed on freight trains, packed in their hundreds and thousands into cattle wagons, and transported to death camps – Treblinka, Sobibor, Majdanek, Belzec, Chelmno and Auschwitz – names which would haunt the lives of an entire post-war generation.

The war
of the rats

Stalingrad, August 1942 – February 1943

Despite their failure to conquer Russia, the Nazi invaders still met with remarkable success. In the summer of 1942, the German army commanded huge swathes of the country. So much, in fact, that before the war 40% of Russia's population had lived in the areas the Germans now occupied. To the north, they had reached the city of Leningrad close to the Finnish border, and continued down past Moscow through the Voronezh front. To the south, they were close to the Volga river, and had got as far as the Caucasus mountains, barely a hundred miles from the Caspian Sea (see map). Millions of Soviet citizens had been killed and millions had fled east. Now, in the late summer of 1942, after more than a year of fighting, the German Sixth Army was fast approaching the industrial city of Stalingrad. Because it was named after Soviet leader Joseph Stalin, the city had great symbolic importance for both the Soviets and the Nazis. Both sides were determined to fight as if the outcome of the entire war depended on their victory. Perhaps it did.

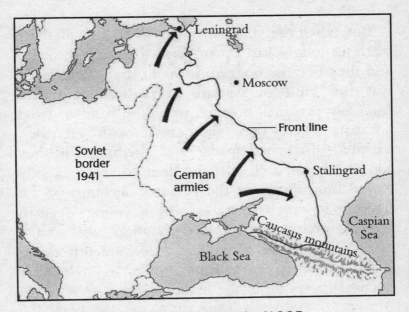

Maximum German penetration into the U.S.S.R. November 1942

The German Sixth Army's arrival at the outskirts of Stalingrad was foreshadowed by a vast cloud of dust thrown up by their marching feet, and the tanks, trucks and artillery that trundled through the parched steppe of late summer. Most of the soldiers, young and still fresh, were in good spirits. The odds were very definitely on their side. Despite occasional heavy fighting, most of those who had trekked the thousand or so miles from the German border to the banks of the Volga had every reason to feel they were as invincible as Nazi propaganda had told them they were. Hitler's armies had astonished the world with their string of victories.

The war of the rats

But, when the Sixth Army got to Stalingrad, there were no longer vast open plains to sweep through, and they became bogged down in street fighting. It was the kind of warfare every soldier dreads. Intensely personal, horrific, terrifying hand-to-hand combat, where men fight men with grenades, bayonets, sharpened spades, and anything else they can grab to kill each other in the most brutal, bloody way. Among many of the personal accounts of the fighting to emerge was one by a young German army lieutenant. His numb description sums up the personal nightmare of Stalingrad so eloquently that it is mentioned in virtually all books and television documentaries about the battle:

"We have fought during fifteen days for a single house. The front is a corridor between burned-out rooms; it is the thin ceiling between two floors … From floor to floor, faces black with sweat, we bombard each other with grenades in the middle of explosions, clouds of dust and smoke, heaps of mortar, floods of blood, fragments of furniture and human beings …The street is no longer measured by dimension but by corpses … Stalingrad is no longer a town. By day it is an enormous cloud of burning, blinding smoke; it is a vast furnace lit by the reflection of the flames. And when night arrives, one of those scorching, howling, bleeding nights, the dogs plunge into the Volga and swim desperately to gain the other bank. The nights of Stalingrad are a terror for them. Animals flee this hell; the hardest stones cannot bear it for long; only men endure."

The battle raged from August 1942 to February 1943, and in such fearful and exhausting circumstances, the morale of each side would be a major deciding factor in the outcome. The Germans arrived convinced that victory would soon be theirs. The Russians fought desperately to cling on to what remained of their front line positions. They were overawed by the German army who, after all, had yet to face a serious defeat. At one point early in the struggle, ninetenths of Stalingrad was in German hands. So confident in victory was the commander of the German Sixth Army,

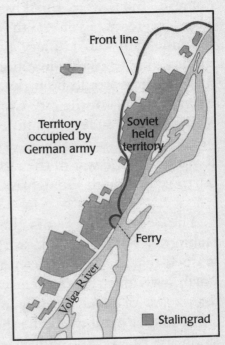

Stalingrad during an early stage of the battle, September 1942

General Friedrich von Paulus, that he had already designed a medal commemorating the capture of the city.

To begin with, the casualty rate among the Soviet army was unsustainable. Reinforcements, rushed to Stalingrad to prop up its crumbling barricades, would arrive at a railhead on the other side of the Volga. They would be bundled out of cattle wagons to be greeted by the terrifying sight of a city in flames. It looked, quite literally, like a vision of hell. From the railhead, men were quickly transferred across the river by ferry. Even if they survived the heavy machine gun and artillery bombardments, and the strafing of the *Stuka* dive bombers as they crossed, these soldiers would be lucky to live for 24 hours.

As each area of the city was overtaken by fighting, Stalingrad was reduced to little more than a huge pile of rubble. German soldiers described the fighting as *Rattenkrieg* - the war of the rats - as men scurried and burrowed through the debris.

The commander of the Russian forces at Stalingrad was General Vassili Chuikov. He quickly grasped that the key to survival in the city would be small, individual encounters with the enemy, rather than a war of tanks, artillery and bombers. The most lethal soldier of all would be the sniper. In the bizarre landscape of the city, with its acres of demolished or burned-out factories and apartment buildings, Stalingrad was perfect sniper territory. A soldier would feel he could be killed at any moment by a sharpshooter perched atop some derelict eyrie. A handful of good snipers could completely demoralize an entire front line regiment. Because of their importance to the defenders, Soviet snipers were rewarded well for their efforts. A marksman with 40 kills, for example, won a medal and the title "noble sniper".

This highly specialized job requires both particular skills and an uncommon personality. It is one thing to kill a soldier when he is charging toward you with a bayonet. It is an entirely different matter to observe him coldly from a hiding place. He may be shaving, chatting to a friend, writing a letter home, or even squatting over a latrine. A sniper must kill him in cold blood, and at the moment when he is least likely to give away his own position. Sniping is a skill which requires great cunning and patience. Especially when one sniper is sent to stalk another. A sound knowledge of camouflage is essential. At Stalingrad, skilled snipers learned to fire against a white background, where the flash of their rifle shot could be less easily seen. Some snipers improvised special attachments to their rifles, which hid the flash of a shot. Some set up dummy figures to act as lures, returning to them regularly to move their position.

Early September was a particularly desperate time in the battle. It was then that Vasily Zaitsev, a sniper of the Russian 62nd Army, began to make a name for himself. In his first 10 days in the city, he managed to kill 40 German soldiers. Zaitsev was a 22-year-old shepherd from the Elininski forest of the Ural mountains. He had learned to shoot as a young boy, and was already a skilled marksman before he even joined the army. He had the broad, open face of a

Russian peasant. All of this made him ideal material for Soviet propaganda newspapers. Such papers were desperately trying to instill some confidence and fighting spirit into the soldiers of the city. Zaitsev's combination of ordinariness and special talent made him a perfect "people's hero". Even his name was just right – Zaitsev is a surname derived from the Russian word for "hare". Animal cunning and speed were perfect attributes for a sniper. As his fame grew, his story was also taken up by national newspapers, newsreels and radio broadcasts.

Such was his success, the army had Zaitsev set up a sniper training school close to the front. Here, between forays to the German front lines, he passed on his skills to eager recruits. "Conceal yourself like a stone," he told them. "Observe, study the terrain, compile a chart and plot distinctive marks on it. Remember that if in the process of observation you have revealed yourself to the enemy... you will receive a bullet through your head." He taught his pupils how to use dummies, and other ruses, to lure enemy snipers into giving away their position. Sometimes he would taunt an opponent with a firing range target. Then, when he was confident he had discovered his enemy's hiding place, he would hurry back to where his dummy had been, and swiftly catch his opponent off guard. Snipers sometimes played these games with each other. Zaitsev warned his pupils never to become angry at such tactics. The way to stay alive as a sniper was to "look before you leap".

A sniper needed to be intimately familiar with the territory in which he operated. Anything different, a pile of bricks here, a slightly-shifted pile of wooded planks there, would tell an experienced soldier that an enemy sniper lay hidden and waiting for his next victim.

Among Zaitsev's pupils was a young woman named Tania Chernova. Like many Russian women, she fought as a front line soldier. Several of her family had been killed in the war, and Tania had a deep hatred for her enemy. She always called them "sticks" – targets – refusing even to think of them as human beings. She had a special skill as a sniper, and often fought alongside Zaitsev. Sharing the hardships of front line soldiers, they snatched meals eaten with a spoon kept in their boots, bathed in buckets of cold water, and slept huddled together in dark overcrowded shelters. As courtships went it was hardly flowers and candle-lit dinners, but in the intense atmosphere of the front, where death was often an instant away, the two became lovers.

From their careful monitoring of the Soviet newspapers and radio broadcasts, and their interrogations of captured Soviet soldiers, the Germans soon learned about Vasily Zaitsev. His worth to the Russians as a morale booster was obvious. The German Sixth Army high command also realized what a prize it would be to kill him. Besides, the success of Soviet snipers was making life so unpleasant for the German ground troops, that no one dared raise their head above the rubble in the hours of daylight.

An SS Colonel named Heinz Thorwald, head of the sniper training school at Zossen, near Berlin, was flown to Stalingrad to dispatch Zaitsev. He had several advantages over the Soviet sniper. He knew all about the techniques of his opponent, because Soviet newspapers and army training leaflets full of this information had been passed on to him. Zaitsev, on the other hand, knew nothing about him – although he had been tipped off that the Germans had sent one of their best snipers to kill him. For several days he kept his eyes and ears open for any clues as to the whereabouts of this Nazi "super-sniper", as Zaitsev called him. Then, in a single day, his friend Morozov was killed and another comrade, Shaikin, was badly wounded. Both men were expert snipers. They had been outfoxed by someone of even greater talent.

Zaitsev hurried to the section of the front line where his comrades had been shot – the Red October factory district, a malignant landscape of twisted machinery and the skeletal framework of partially demolished buildings. Like a police inspector investigating a murder, he asked soldiers who had witnessed the shootings exactly what had happened, and where his comrades had been hit. Making use of his now considerable experience, he deduced that the shots had to come from a position directly in front of the area where these men had fallen. Across the lines, amid the tangled rubble, was the hulk of a burned-out tank. This was too obvious a spot for an experienced sniper. To the right of the tank was an abandoned concrete pillbox. But the firing slit there had been boarded up. Between these two landmarks, right in front of Zaitsev's own position, was a sheet of corrugated iron lying amid piles of bricks. This, he thought, was the perfect place for a sniper to hide, then crawl away under cover of darkness.

As he studied the landscape, Zaitsev caught sight of the top of a helmet moving along the edge of an enemy trench, and instinctively reached for his rifle. But then he realized, by the way the helmet was wobbling along, that this was a trap. Colonel Thorwald almost certainly had an assistant who had placed the helmet on a stick and was waiting for Zaitsev to reveal his position by firing at this dummy target.

Putting his theory to the test, Zaitsev placed a glove on a small plank and raised it above a brick parapet in front of the iron sheeting. At once a shot rang out, piercing the glove and plank in an instant. Zaitsev looked at his plank carefully. The bullet had gone straight through it. His quarry was obviously directly under the iron sheet.

After dark, Zaitsev and his friend Kulikov scouted the area for suitable firing spots. The night wore on with occasional bursts of rifle fire, followed by sporadic mortar and artillery barrages. Every now and then a flare would shoot high into the air in a graceful arc, floating down in a bright blaze that cast harsh shadows over the still, sinister landscape.

When the sun rose the next morning it fell directly on them, so they waited. To have fired then, with the sunlight catching their rifles or telescopic sights, would have been too risky. But, by early afternoon, the sun had moved across the sky, and over to the German lines. At the edge of the iron sheet, something glistened in the bright light. Was it Thorwald's rifle, or just a piece of broken glass? Kulikov offered the German sniper a target. Very carefully he raised his helmet above the broken brick wall they sheltered behind. A shot rang out, piercing the metal helmet. Kulikov rose slightly and screamed, as if he had been hit. Unable to contain his curiosity Thorwald raised his head a little from behind the iron sheet, to try to get a better look. It was the chance Zaitsev had been waiting for. He fired a single shot, and Thorwald's head fell back. That night, Zaitsev crept up to his opponent's position to take his rifle as a souvenir. You can still see the telescopic sight on display at the Armed Forces Museum in Moscow.

The course of the battle of Stalingrad makes up one of the great horror stories of modern history. The Germans, together with their Italian, Hungarian and Romanian allies, lost 850,000 men. The Soviets lost 750,000. But Stalingrad was not just the scene of a vast, prolonged battle, it was also a city of half a million people. In the first two days of the fighting, 40,000 of them were killed in German bombing raids. By the end, a mere 1,500 were still alive among the rubble, although some who had lived in the city before the Germans came had already fled to other parts of Russia.

The battle ended when Soviet forces outside Stalingrad surrounded the Germans, cutting them off inside the city. "There is not a single healthy man left at the front...everyone is at least suffering from frostbite," ran a report by Sixth Army commanders to Berlin on January 18, 1943. "The commander of the 76th Infantry Division on a visit to the front yesterday came across many soldiers who had frozen to death." But Hitler refused to allow his starving, demoralized Sixth Army to give in. Von Paulus and his troops went through a further two weeks of needless suffering before he defied direct orders and submitted to the Russians. Of the 91,000 Germans who surrendered, only 5,000 would ever return home. The rest died in captivity.

Sad to say, there was to be no happy ending to the relationship between Vasily Zaitsev and Tania Chernova. Shortly after Zaitsev survived his encounter with Colonel Thorwald, Tania was critically wounded. She and a small squad of soldiers had been sent out to assassinate von Paulus. On the way to the German front lines, one of them stepped on a mine. In the explosion, Tania received a near fatal stomach wound. Zaitsev was told she was not expected to live. But Tania survived. Several months later, while recovering in a hospital in Tashkent, far behind the front lines, she too received terrible news. Zaitsev had been killed in an explosion in the final weeks of fighting in Stalingrad. Sunk in despair, for weeks afterwards she would just stare into space. Eventually she recovered her health and even married, although the wound she received meant that she could never have children. For Tania, like so many others, the war had consequences she would have to bear for the rest of her life.

Only in 1969, when she was in her late 40s, did she learn that Zaitsev was still alive. After the war he had married, and became the director of an engineering school. It was bittersweet news, because she still loved him. The explosion she had been told about had happened. Zaitsev had also been caught by a mine. It had blinded him temporarily, but he too had recovered.

Note

The identity of Colonel Thorwald is a thorny historical issue. In some accounts he is referred to as Major Koning or Konig. Zaitsev wrote about the duel described here in his post-war memoirs, but does not mention his rival by name. No one doubts Zaitsev's skill and achievements as a sniper, but some historians think the episode with Thorwald/Konig was made up, or at least heavily embroidered, by Soviet propagandists. The story about Tania Chernova is undoubtedly true, and was taken directly from her personal experience of the battle of Stalingrad given to American historian William Craig in his book 'Enemy at the Gates'.

The lost hero

Raoul Wallenberg in Hungary, 1944-1945

Hatred and persecution of the Jews in Germany, and the territories the Nazis conquered, was common knowledge during the war. But what was not known almost until the war ended was that random murder had turned into full scale genocide. Then, in 1944, two Jews named Rudolf Vrba and Alfred Wetzler escaped from Auschwitz – a massive concentration and extermination camp in Poland. They compiled a report giving clear details of the gas chambers – the final destination of Jews swept up in the mass deportations that followed the Wannsee Conference. Their report added to mounting evidence confirming the unthinkable – the Nazis were setting out to murder every single Jew in Europe.

When British prime minister Winston Churchill read the report in July 1944 he wrote, "This is the greatest, most horrible crime ever committed in the whole history of the world." American president Franklin Roosevelt had already established the U.S. War Refugee Board with the intention of funding any neutral states prepared to offer help to the Jews. Now he issued a proclamation to all of the Axis powers, warning them that they would be held personally responsible if they supported the Nazis in their persecution of the Jews. But really there was little practical that the Allies could do to stop the rail deportations and mass killings. They were, after all, being carried out far behind the front lines. A resentful debate still continues to this day regarding measures the Allies could have taken to hinder the Nazi's "Final Solution".

While Vrba and Wetzler's Auschwitz report was circulating in government departments in Washington and London, the Nazis began to round up the 850,000 Jews in Hungary. Until early 1944, they had been protected by the Hungarian government. The leader of Hungary, Admiral Miklós Horthy was a supporter and ally of Hitler's, but he had no sympathy for the Nazis' anti-Semitism, and even spoke out against what he called the "inhuman, cruel persecution of the Jews". But, in March 1944, Hitler became suspicious that the Hungarians might make a separate peace with the Allies, and sent German troops to occupy the country. The Nazis allowed Horthy to stay as leader, to give the impression that the Hungarians were still in charge of their own destiny. Even so, Hungarian Jews immediately became the target for violent, often fatal, attacks. Adolf Eichmann and SS troops arrived, to organize the deportation of the Jewish population.

Between May and July, Eichmann worked with great efficiency. Some 437,000 Jews were rounded up, packed into freight trains, and sent to Auschwitz (see the map on page 88). Of this number at least 365,000 were killed. By midsummer the lives of the remaining Jews left in Hungary were hanging by a thread. Not only were the German troops after them, but Hungary had its own brand of anti-Semitic fascists too, known as the Arrow Cross. This militaristic organization was a strange brew of fanatical Catholics and pro-Nazi supporters, and they attacked Hungarian Jews with as much zeal as the Nazis.

Word of these deportations soon reached the Allies. The United States appealed to neutral nations with legations (diplomatic offices) or embassies in Budapest, the Hungarian capital. They could help by granting some kind of protective status to Hungary's Jews. The Swedish legation issued "protective passes", which declared that the holder should be treated as if he or she were a Swedish citizen. Swedish diplomats stationed in the United States offered more direct help. They recommended a 32-year-old businessman named Raoul Wallenberg to act as a special emissary to help the Jews of Hungary.

Wallenberg came from a long line of bankers, diplomats, politicians and military men, in one of the most famous families in Sweden. He was born in August 1912, three months after his navy father died of cancer. He was a curious character – a sensitive, gentle soul who was also quite fearless. As a child he hated fox hunting and once let all the dogs on the family estate escape on the night before a hunt. His family had intended him to become a banker, but Wallenberg was more interested in architecture and trade. He trained as an architect at Michigan University in the United States. His girlfriend there worked with physically handicapped children, and he would often help look after her pupils.

In the 1930s, Wallenberg worked for a while in Haifa, in Palestine, where he met Jewish refugees fleeing from the Nazis. Returning to Sweden, he set up a successful food import and export business, the Mid European Trading Company, with a Jewish Hungarian partner named Koloman Lauer. When the Second World War broke out, Sweden remained neutral. This meant Wallenberg was able to travel around Germany, her allies and conquered territory as he wished, cutting business deals with Nazi officials and their collaborators. His work often took him to Budapest.

Wallenberg was more than happy to help, and set off for Hungary at once by train. He reached the capital on July 9, 1944, arriving with $100,000 donated by American Jewish charities to fund his activities. Although he knew what the Germans intended to do to the Jews, he also understood the bizarre mentality of most Nazi officials. The men who ruled Germany and its conquered territories had such warped priorities that destroying the Jews was often more important to them than delaying or defeating the approaching Soviet army. But, at the same time, these same men were usually so corrupt that they were also quite open to whatever bribes Wallenberg could put their way. It was a strange combination, but it created a small corridor of opportunity in which Wallenberg could operate.

Because he had made plenty of business trips to occupied Europe, he also understood how to handle the "little people". He knew that ordinary soldiers and policemen had a deep fear and exaggerated respect for authority. Wallenberg had an inherent advantage. He was tall and well-spoken, and in several languages too, including German, Russian and English. As a wealthy aristocrat from a prominent Swedish family, he had a natural air of authority, which he could use to his benefit. Here in Budapest, he was the perfect example of a man and his circumstances matching perfectly. His sensitivity, his plain decency, his keen knowledge of human character and quick-thinking intelligence all allowed him to survive in what would soon become a treacherous madhouse.

With the help of other Swedish diplomats, Wallenberg immediately set about manufacturing a fictitious Swedish citizenship document called a Schutzpass, meaning a "protective pass". The Swedes in Budapest had already made similar passes, but Wallenberg's design was a major improvement.

Knowing how much both the Nazis and the Hungarians admired impressive-looking documents, Wallenberg cooked up a formidable-looking pass in blue and yellow. It had coats of arms, official stamps, signatures, and the three crown symbol of Sweden. He was given permission to manufacture 5,000 of these passes but actually made 15,000 of them. Other meaningless identification documents were also created, to wave at guards and policemen to convince them that the bearer should be left alone. Such passes declared that the holder was emigrating to Sweden, and was a Swedish citizen, and that the protection offered by the pass should also be extended to the holder's family.

Shortly after Wallenberg arrived in Hungary, he came across Adolf Eichmann. They arranged to meet in a nightclub in Budapest in early August. Here Wallenberg offered to buy a substantial amount of Nazi-owned property in the capital. Eichmann knew that he wanted these buildings to provide sanctuary for Jews, and so he brushed aside his offer. He was unimpressed with Wallenberg, dismissing him as a "soft... and decadent diplomat".

At the time, Eichmann was meeting resistance to his deportations from several quarters. Although Horthy no longer had the power he had wielded before German troops took over his country, he was still making some efforts to protect Hungarian Jews. Various factions within the Nazi party were also squabbling about how and when to carry out the deportations, which delayed their implementation as well. As a result, the deportations were put on hold, and Eichmann returned to Germany.

By early autumn Wallenberg's efforts to protect Hungarian Jews had been so successful he was contemplating returning home. But events took a turn for the worse. Admiral Horthy had become convinced that Hungary should withdraw from the war. So, on October 15, a pre-recorded speech by him was broadcast on Hungarian national radio, announcing the end of the war as far as Hungary was concerned. The speech was greeted with delight, and people danced in the streets. But Horthy had underestimated the ruthless determination of his Nazi allies. Minutes after the broadcast had finished, another announcement was made, claiming Hungary was still at war. Suddenly, the airwaves were filled with the sound of Nazi marching songs. This almost instant change of heart was brought in part because SS troops had kidnapped Horthy's son. They threatened to execute him unless the Admiral changed his mind. Horthy stepped down as leader, and went into exile in Bavaria. His son was sent to a concentration camp. The fascist Arrow Cross party took control of the country, under the leadership of Ferenc Szálasi.

Szálasi's government immediately announced they would no longer recognize the Swedish Schutzpasses. But Wallenberg had a trick up his sleeve. He was friendly with a young Austrian aristocrat named Liesel Kemény, who had recently married the new Hungarian foreign minister. Wallenberg told Kemény that the Jews were being deported to be exterminated. If her new husband allowed this to happen he would be hanged after the war as part of a government that had permitted such an atrocity to take place. Madame Kemény talked her husband into persuading the new government to recognize the Schutzpass after all.

But, with Horthy gone, armed thugs of the Arrow Cross were unleashed to murder Jews on the streets. Eichmann and his SS troops returned. Jewish community leaders were summoned to a meeting with him. "You see I am back again," Eichmann hissed at them, like some pantomime villain. "You forget Hungary is still in the shadow of the Reich. My arms are long and I can reach the Jews of Budapest as well." The deportations began again. At this stage of the war, the massive resources that had been available to the Nazis in the initial stages of the Final Solution were no longer theirs to command. The Russians were fast approaching from the east, cutting rail links. Fuel, locomotives and freight wagons were scarce. But Eichmann's determination was undimmed. When trains could not be found to transport the Jews, they were marched out of Budapest instead.

With the Arrow Cross to help him, Eichmann worked fast. In a few dark autumn days, 80,000 Jews were rounded up in Budapest and marched out of the capital to Austria. Jews deported from Budapest usually went straight to Auschwitz, but this group was earmarked to be worked to death in armament factories. If anyone faltered on the march, they were shot where they dropped, and many others simply froze to death during overnight stops, or died from plain exhaustion. But, whenever columns of Jews were marched off, Wallenberg soon followed after them with food and medical supplies. He would hand out protective passes, and always managed to bring back a few hundred people from the thousands who left.

His bravery on these occasions was extraordinary. He would rush into a crowd of frightened Jews assembled for deportation, right under the bayonets and rifles of jittery, ill-tempered guards. Then he would shout, "Who here has Swedish papers?", while handing them out to those around him. Sometimes, Wallenberg arrived when a train packed with Jews was due to depart for Auschwitz. He would stand in front of the locomotive to prevent it from leaving, then clamber down the roof of the freight carriages, handing out his Schutzpasses to any hands that appeared through the narrow slats at the sides. Sometimes he would just stuff bundles of passes into the trains. Occasionally, he would be roughly manhandled by the guards, or have warning shots fired above his head. Wallenberg had no official right to behave as he did. But he always acted as if he had complete authority, and was a man whose orders should not be disobeyed.

It was in early November that Wallenberg met Eichmann again face to face, this time at *Gestapo* headquarters in Budapest. Eichmann greeted his mild-mannered opponent with open hostility and plain threats, but was taken aback when Wallenberg presented him with a gift of Scotch whiskey and cigarettes. Unlike many Nazi chiefs, Eichmann was not someone who could be bribed. But the shrewd Wallenberg had correctly guessed that the vanity of a man from his humble background would be tickled by a gift from a Swedish aristocrat. The two men shared a drink and Eichmann became quite friendly, even offering to let a small trainload of Jews leave for Sweden, in exchange for a ransom. But Wallenberg knew he couldn't be trusted, and Eichmann's feelings toward him rapidly turned murderous. A few days after the meeting, a German military vehicle attempted to ram Wallenberg's car. It failed. But, thereafter, Wallenberg made a point of regularly changing the house where he slept.

Using money provided by the U.S. War Refugee Board, an "international ghetto" was set up. Rows of houses were bought, 72 in all, and over 15,000 Jews sheltered in them. Sometimes Jewish men who looked particularly "Aryan" (see page 84), dressed in stolen SS uniforms to stand guard outside the houses. Following Wallenberg's example, diplomats from Spain, Portugal and Switzerland also provided safe havens and passes too, renting buildings that would become hiding places for Jews.

Throughout November, as the cold central European winter settled on the capital, the deportations and killings continued. With Russian troops fast approaching, an air of anarchy overtook Budapest, and any semblance of law and order evaporated. Nazi troops and Arrow Cross thugs knew their days were numbered. In their twisted ideology, the Jews were considered the source of all their troubles, and in their final days of power they worked all hours to kill as many as could be found. Houses that were supposedly safe Swedish legation territory were broken into at random, and those sheltering inside were slaughtered.

During this time Eichmann declared: "I know the war is lost, but I am still going to win my war." Despite the obvious attempts Eichmann had made on his life, Wallenberg still thought it was worth inviting him to dinner in a final bid to dissuade him from continuing. So, in mid–December, Wallenberg and Eichmann had their last encounter. A meeting was duly arranged and they, and other dinner guests, met in an imposing hilltop mansion overlooking Budapest.

It was a strangely theatrical evening. Fine food and wines were served on elegant china dishes, and a surprisingly cordial atmosphere was established. After the meal the guest retired to the sitting room for coffee and brandy. The room had a fantastic view over the city. In a well-documented scene that could have come from a Hollywood movie, Wallenberg pulled back the curtains, revealing a horizon lit up with flashes of artillery and rockets from the approaching Soviet army.

"Look how close the Soviets are," Wallenberg said to Eichmann. "Your war is almost over. The Nazis are doomed, finished, and so are those who cling to this hatred until the very last. It's the end of the Nazis, the end of Hitler, the end of Eichmann."

Here, in a moment of cold-blooded frankness that would have shamed the Devil, Eichmann replied, "I agree with you. I've never agreed with all of Hitler's ideology, but it has, after all, given me a good career… Soon, this comfortable life will end. No more planes bringing women and wine from France. The Russians will take my horses, my dogs, and my palace… They'd probably shoot me on the spot. For me there's no escape, no liberation. There are, however, some consolations. If I continue to eliminate our enemies to the end, it may delay our defeat… and then, when I finally walk to the gallows, at least I'll know I've completed my mission."

The Germans left soon after. Eichmann thanked Wallenberg for "an exceptionally charming and interesting evening". Then he sneered, "Now don't think we're friends. We're not. I plan to do everything I can to keep you from saving your Jews. Your diplomatic passport won't protect you from everything. Even a neutral diplomat can meet with an accident."

By Christmas Eve, Russian troops were at the gates of Budapest. Eichmann fled, but his final order was for the remaining 70,000 Jews of Budapest to be rounded up and executed. So, August Schmidthuber, the German general charged with the task of defending the capital, mustered 500 of his men and armed them with heavy machine guns. But Wallenberg was alerted to the forthcoming massacre. He sent word to Schmidthuber that he would hold him personally responsible and see to it that he was hanged as a war criminal when the war ended. The massacre was called off just minutes before it was due to begin. Wallenberg had won probably his greatest victory.

Two days later, on January 13, Soviet troops began to arrive in the outskirts of Budapest. Wallenberg was ecstatic, and convinced his troubles were over. For months he had risked his life and, against extraordinary odds, he had survived. But only when he came up against a supposed friendly army did his luck desert him. His naiveté, which had allowed him to act with such bravery, betrayed him.

Wallenberg had great plans for post-war Budapest, and he outlined to Soviet officers an idea he had to help the Jews after the war. He was invited to discuss matters further behind the Russian lines, and drove away from the capital with a Red Army escort. His friends in Budapest and Sweden never saw him again.

What happened next has been the source of much speculation. Even today, nearly 60 years later, the precise truth is still uncertain. The most likely explanation was that the Russians thought Wallenberg was an American spy. He was arrested and held in a cell – probably in the infamous Lubyanka prison in Moscow, home of the much-feared Soviet secret police.

His best chance of a return home seems to have come in 1946, when the outgoing Swedish ambassador in Moscow was summoned for a final meeting with Soviet dictator Joseph Stalin. Stalin asked him if he had any special requests. In reply the ambassador asked that if Raoul Wallenberg was in Soviet hands, perhaps they could see to it that he was released. But then, tragically, the ambassador admitted to Stalin that he thought Wallenberg was dead. He may as well have signed Wallenberg's death sentence. Stalin was no less ruthless than Hitler. If the Swedes thought Wallenberg was dead, it would be far simpler just to kill him than to admit he had been wrongly imprisoned. Today, the most reliable records available indicate that Wallenberg was executed in his Moscow cell on July 17, 1947.

While Wallenberg had devoted his life to thwarting the evil work of a dying regime, another set of circumstances conspired against him. History would show him to be one of the first victims of the Cold War – the sullen peace between the Soviets and the Western Allies that followed the defeat of Nazi Germany. The war produced more than its fair share of senseless moments, but for a man who had saved anything up to 100,000 lives through sheer bare-knuckle courage, it was a desperately unjust fate.

"...like running through rain and not getting wet."

Iwo Jima, February-March 1945

The photograph that greeted American newspaper readers on the Sunday morning of February 25, 1945, would become one of the most famous images of World War Two. It shows a cluster of six U.S. Marines, their uniforms stained and dusty from three days continual combat, raising a fluttering Stars and Stripes on a long iron pole. The shot catches them in such a classic pose – pole at 45°, their bodies straining with the heavy weight and biting wind, one man crouching at the base, others reaching up as the pole is raised beyond their grasp – the image seemed to echo heroic marble figures in a Roman statue. But photographer Joe Rosenthal, who took the picture, did not even look in his viewfinder when he captured this particular moment of history. It was a lucky fluke.

A reader who scrutinized the shot would get the impression that the men were atop some barren hill, for a pale horizon could be dimly seen below them. The hill was Mount Suribachi on the Japanese island of Iwo Jima, 1,045km (650 miles) south of Tokyo. It was the first piece of Japanese territory to be invaded in 4,000 years.

The story that accompanied the photo told how the men in the shot had struggled up Iwo Jima's Mount Suribachi in the teeth of fierce fire from fanatical Japanese defenders, who rolled grenades down the mountain to explode among them with devastating effect. Then, overcoming ferocious opposition, the Marines raised their flag in a hail of deadly sniper fire. But it was all a work of fiction. To start with, the Stars and Stripes had been raised earlier that day, and the flag in the famous shot was a replacement. It was bigger than the original, which had been quickly removed as a regimental souvenir. The men who planted the flag had walked up the hill unopposed. Why journalists felt the need to manufacture such a story is a mystery, for the actual events at Iwo Jima were far more heroic and harrowing than any overblown propaganda report.

Pacific islands conjure comforting images of white sand, blue sea and sunshine. Not Iwo Jima. It is a bleak volcanic slab of black ash and scrubby vegetation, shaped like an overloaded ice cream cone, and frequently lashed with driving rain. The name means "sulphur island"*. That evil-smelling chemical similar to rotten eggs, emanates from the dormant volcano that makes up the glowering hillside at its southern tip. The island is so small, 20 square km (8

*"Sulphur" is spelled "sulfur" in the United States.

square miles), that it only takes five or six minutes to drive across it.

During the war, many Pacific islands inhabited by Japanese soldiers were simply cut off from supplies by the allies, and left to starve or surrender. But Iwo Jima was a notable exception. Its importance lay in two Japanese air force bases inland from its stone and ash beaches. From here fighter planes scythed into the huge, silver U.S. *B-29* bombers that passed daily back and forth to pound the factories and cities of mainland Japan. Iwo Jima, in American hands, would provide these bombers with a base closer to Japan, especially one for emergency landings on their return journey.

The battle at Iwo Jima was one of the fiercest, and certainly the most famous, of the war in the Pacific. On one side were the soldiers of Imperial Japan. Since

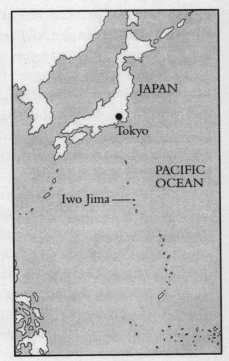

Map showing location of Iwo Jima

the 1930s, they had been fighting to build a Japanese empire in the Pacific – conquering territories that were once part of the empires of fading European powers. These soldiers fought with suicidal bravery and infamous cruelty. They had only contempt for enemy soldiers who surrendered when defeat seemed inevitable. Even when facing certain capture, most would kill themselves rather than fall into enemy hands.

On the other side was the United States. Like their Japanese counterparts, American soldiers fought with unquestionable bravery, but it was not part of their culture to sacrifice themselves needlessly if defeat was inevitable. America had been at war with Japan since 1941, when the Japanese naval air service had launched a ferocious surprise attack on the American fleet at its Hawaiian base in Pearl Harbor. The architect of this attack, Admiral Yamamoto Isoroku, was never convinced of its wisdom. "I fear we have only succeeded in awakening a sleeping tiger," he said in response to congratulations following its success. Yamamoto was right. The United States was the richest, most powerful nation on Earth. Once war broke out, President Roosevelt devoted the entire resources of his country to winning it. The invasion fleet sent to attack Iwo Jima was an extraordinary 110km (70 miles) long. Aboard its 800 warships were over 300,000 men, a third of whom were intended to fight on the island itself.

The Japanese knew the strength of their enemy all

too well. Many senior soldiers and diplomats had visited or lived in America before the war. The commander of Iwo Jima, Lieutenant General Tadamichi Kuribayashi, was one of them. His strategy in defending his tiny island was grimly effective. His orders to his 21,000 soldiers were brutally frank. They were outnumbered and outgunned, with no hope of rescue. The island was sure to fall – eventually. But they had a sacred duty to defend this Japanese territory to the death. Every man was instructed to kill at least ten Americans before he died. Kuribayashi, and his masters in Japan, knew that American troops were heading inexorably toward the mainland, intent on conquering their country. They hoped that American losses on Iwo Jima would be so appalling that the American public would force President Roosevelt to come to a compromise peace with Japan, so preventing an invasion, and the resulting national humiliation.

So, in the months before the invasion, Iwo Jima was turned into a formidable fortress. Pillboxes and concrete gun emplacements littered the island. Every cave held a unit of soldiers, and linking them all up was an intricate network of tunnels. There were even underground hospitals large enough to treat 400 wounded men. Japanese soldiers were not on Iwo Jima; they were in it. "No other given area in the history of modern war has been so skillfully fortified by nature and by man," stated one post-war report.

The soldiers sent to seize this tiny island were from

the 3rd, 4th, 5th and 21st divisions of the U.S. Marines, under the overall command of Lt. General Holland M. "Howling Mad" Smith. The Marines Corps prided themselves on their skill at seaborne assaults, and their fierce fighting spirit and intense loyalty. But the majority of those sent to Iwo Jima had never been in combat before. Most, in fact, were boys of 18 or 19. They were fated to be thrown into the most savage of battles at an age when many other young men would be grappling with their final year in high school, first year at college, first job, first love... most had not even left home. Some were even younger – boys of 16 and 17 who had lied about their age when they were recruited. It was little wonder that when such boys died at the point of a Japanese bayonet, or blown in half by shell or mortar, their veneer of manly toughness seared away, their last words were often a frantic, desperate cry to their mothers.

The attack began on the morning of February 19. A pink winter sunrise and pale blue sky greeted the thousands of Marines aboard the invasion fleet. They had spent a sleepless night in preparation for the assault, and their day began at 3:00am, when they were all heartily fed with steak and eggs for breakfast. Then, around 7:00am, they filed off their vast, troop carrying boats, down metal steps to fill the holds of the smaller landing craft that would take them to the island. Here, one boy who had never been in combat,

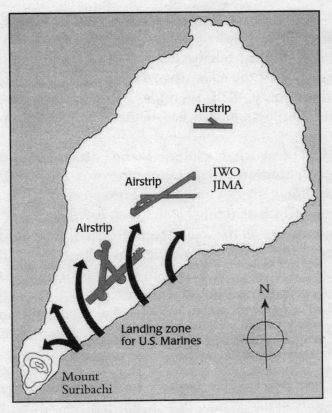

The U.S. assault on Iwo Jima

recalled some sardonic advice he received from an older soldier. "You don't know what's going to happen. You're going to learn more in the first five minutes there than you did in the whole year of training you've been through."

The naval shelling of the island stopped at 8:57am. Five minutes later, clumsy amphibious tanks emerged from landing craft onto the soft beaches which ran

125

for 3km (two miles) down the south side of the island. They trundled directly underneath the baleful gaze of Mount Suribachi. Such was the operational efficiency of the U.S. navy, the invasion was only an extraordinary 120 seconds behind the carefully planned schedule that had begun when the fleet left Hawaii.

The fear that clutched the hearts of troops approaching an enemy shoreline was intense. Each man knew that when the heavy steel door at the front of his landing craft was lowered into the frothing sea at the edge of the beach, he could be exposed to lacerating machine gun fire. That is, if he hadn't already been blown to pieces by a shell before his boat even reached the shore.

Yet when the doors of the first wave of landing craft went down at Iwo Jima, the Marines were greeted only by the corrosive smell of sulphur. Although shells from their ships and planes were whistling over their heads and on to the island, the Japanese themselves were eerily silent. At first many soldiers assumed the relentless 74-day bombardment of the island by U.S. bombers, navy battleships and carrier aircraft, had wiped out the island's defenders. But Kuribayashi had ordered his men to hold their fire while the beach filled up with American troops, tanks and supplies. When the Japanese bombardment began an hour after the U.S. invasion, it was catastrophic.

Amid the chaos of disembarking tanks, and

bulldozers whose caterpillar tracks churned up the soft sand, hordes of wet, bewildered men milled around the beach. Then these men became aware of another more terrible distraction. All at once a lethal rain of shells, bullets and mortar fire fell upon them. One officer recalled that Mount Suribachi suddenly lit up like a Christmas tree – only, instead of lights and tinsel, the flashes he could see were gun and shellfire. The whole mountainside had been turned into a fortress, seven stories of fire platforms and gun emplacements, all hollowed out of its interior.

There was nowhere to hide. Marines hugged the soft sand as bullets flew over them so low they ripped the clothes and supplies in their backpacks to shreds. The carnage was hideous. Men were torn apart by shells, their bodies spread over the beach, causing even hardened veterans to vomit in horror. Others, caught directly by high explosive shells, were simply vaporized, and left no trace of human remains.

One Marine novice, having no real idea how this compared with other battles, yelled over to his commander. "Hey, Sergeant… is this a bad battle?" The sergeant shouted back, "It's a ★★★★★★★ slaughter." A minute later the sergeant was blown to pieces by a mortar. Press photographer Joe Rosenthal was on the beach that day. "…not getting hit was like running through rain and not getting wet," he remembered. Another Marine, Lloyd Keeland, recalled: "I think your life expectancy was about 20 seconds…"

In that first hour of shelling the success of the invasion hung in the balance. But although it took a terrible toll, there were too many Marines already there, and too many still coming ashore, to wipe them off the island.

There were several things about the fighting on Iwo Jima that made it especially horrific. Such was the intensity of the Japanese bombardment that it didn't matter whether a soldier crouched in a foxhole or charged through open land. He would be killed either way. Another was that the enemy was completely invisible. Often, American soldiers only saw their Japanese adversaries when they were dead. For the rest of the time, Marines were fired upon by an unseen foe who could all too clearly see them.

Once off the beach, Marines headed into thin scrub and grasses, and terrain peppered with blockhouses, pillboxes, caves and rocks – almost all of which held or sheltered Japanese soldiers. Every one had to be attacked, and every one caused some casualties, before a hail of machine gun bullets, or a grenade or flame-thrower put an end to its defenders. But, more often than not, it didn't. The tunnel system that linked the Japanese strongpoints meant that a "neutralized" blockhouse could quickly become a lethal one again, with Japanese soldiers who had crawled through the tunnels, shooting at the backs of unsuspecting Marines.

Yet, despite the slaughter, the Marines were

winning. The dreadful opening bombardment had not driven them off the beach, and by noon 9,000 men had come ashore. Even by mid-morning, one company from the 28th Marine Regiment had managed to cross the 650m (700 yards) that separated the furthest southern landing beach from the island's western shore. Their casualties were daunting – of the 250 men in the company, only 37 were still standing.

As night fell, the fighting subsided. 30,000 men had managed to come ashore. But as exhausted Marines lay huddled in shallow holes and trenches, they were assailed by Japanese soldiers, who sneaked out one by one to claim an unwary life before melting away into the darkness.

The next dawn brought fierce winds and high seas – making further landings difficult. As other Marine forces began cautiously to infiltrate the northern interior of the island, the great plan for the day was to attack Suribachi itself. The task was given to Colonel Harry "the Horse" Liversedge, and the 3,000 Marines of his 28th Regiment. All that day, they edged up to the base of the mountain.

The weather on the third morning on the island brought no respite. It was a grim day to die. As the 28th Marine Regiment prepared for its assault on Suribachi, a Marine artillery barrage from behind their lines opened up for an hour. Then U.S. carrier planes swooped in to plaster the mountain with rockets. But the designated hour of the attack,

8:00am, came and went without the order being given to advance. Colonel Liversedge had been promised tanks to protect his men as they ran through open ground toward the tangle of vegetation that covered the base of Suribachi. Without tanks, his losses would be far worse than he was already expecting. But the tanks had not arrived. (They were short of fuel and shells, he found out later.) So, Liversedge decided, the attack would have to go on anyway.

When the order was passed around the regiment that they were to charge forward without tanks, raw dread swept through the men. One soldier, Lieutenant Keith Wells, was reminded of the atmosphere in his father's slaughterhouse, when cattle realize they are about to be killed. Showing uncommon courage, Wells led by example. Despite a fear so deep he could feel it as a physical weight bearing down on him, he broke cover and began to run toward the mountain slope. He expected to be cut down in seconds. But, as he ran on, he could see hundreds of other Marines following on behind him, given courage by his bravery. Suribachi erupted into a dazzling flash of fire, and shells and bullets scythed down the charging Marines. But the men had been trained to advance at all costs, and gradually they reached the base of the mountain. Among those wounded was Lieutenant Wells, his legs peppered with shrapnel. His wounds were sufficiently bad to merit pain-killing morphine from a medic who treated him, but Wells still refused to leave his men. He directed them to destroy the blockhouses and machine-gun nests that lay at the foot of Suribachi, until loss of blood made him delirious. Gradually, men with flame-throwers were able to get close enough to do their hideous work. When the tanks eventually appeared to back up the assault, the Japanese front line on the mountain began to crumble at last.

Throughout the day, the companies and platoons of the regiment inched further up the mountain – by nightfall some had even penetrated behind Japanese lines. They lay low amid the parachute flares, and searchlights from offshore ships that combed the mountain with penetrating brilliance, fearing that every moving shadow was an approaching Japanese soldier.

On the fourth day, the Marines continued to creep forward, sometimes hearing their enemy in tunnels and command posts beneath them, but more often than not only locating a Japanese strong point when a hail of fire was unleashed on them. By now the Marines had strong tank and artillery support, and the Japanese inside Suribachi were blown and burned to oblivion. In the fading light, Japanese soldiers, increasingly aware that they were now cut off from any possible retreat, staged a breakout. One hundred and fifty suddenly broke cover, in a desperate dash down the mountain, only to be slaughtered by Marines who were getting their first sight of the soldiers who had visited such torment on them. Only 25 made it back to the Japanese lines.

At the dawn of day five, Liversedge sensed a major morale-raising coup was in his grasp. Although he suspected that many Japanese soldiers probably remained inside Suribachi, their strength as a fighting force was gone, and it might now be possible to capture the mountain outright. If he was wrong, it could prove to be a very costly gamble.

The day's fighting began with another air attack: carrier planes smothered the top of the mountain in napalm. After that, Suribachi seemed oddly quiet. Had all the remaining Japanese fled? There was only one way to find out. A four-man patrol was sent up the mountain's 168m (550ft) summit, each man fearing his life was measured in seconds, and that death was a footstep away. But the enemy never did open fire, and the commanding officer at the base of the mountain, Colonel Chandler Johnson, decided to risk a 40-man platoon. Lieutenant Schrier, the officer given the task of leading these men, was summoned before Colonel Johnson. He gave him a small American flag. "If you get to the top," said Johnson tactlessly, "put it up."

As Schrier's platoon snaked higher up the mountain, they caught the eye of every man on the beach and island close enough to see them. Then word got around. Even those offshore, in the vast armada that surrounded the island, trained their binoculars and telescopes on the thin line of men. At any second, both the platoon and their thousands of spectators expected the remaining Japanese on Suribachi to open up and cut them to ribbons.

The platoon advanced gingerly, and with great caution. At every cave they came to, they tossed in a grenade, in case it contained enemy troops. But, after forty tense minutes, they stood breathless at the top, not quite believing they were still alive. At 10:20am they raised the Stars and Stripes on the summit, using a piece of drainage pipe as a flagpole. When the flag went up, a huge cheer rose from the throats of the thousands of Marines who had been watching below. Offshore, warships sounded their horns, and men onboard hollered in triumph. "Our spirits were very low at that point," recalled one soldier, Hershel "Woody" Williams, "because we had lost so many men and made so little gain. The whole spirit changed." Although the fighting was far from over, seeing the American flag flying over Iwo Jima's highest point convinced every Marine that they were there to stay.

Around the flag, Marines stood uneasily, posing for army photographer Louis Lowery. With the flag fluttering in a strong breeze, and their silhouettes standing out on the top of the mountain, they would soon be the target for every enemy sniper and artilleryman within range. One of the soldiers present recalled, "It was like sitting in the middle of a bull's-eye."

Sure enough, the cacophony touched off by the raising of the flag had alerted the Japanese. The ragged soldiers left on the mountain began to emerge from hiding places. They tossed grenades or loosed off a few rounds toward the Marines, who dived for cover and began to fight back. But, amazingly, no one was hurt, and soon the mountain settled down again to a sullen silence.

There were indeed still several hundred Japanese troops left on Suribachi, but they had lost the will to carry on. Strange as it seemed to the American Marines, most chose to kill themselves rather than fight to the death or surrender.

Watching the flag-raising from the beach below was "Howling Mad" Smith, and none other than the U.S. Secretary of the Navy James Forrestal, a man so important that he would later have a large aircraft carrier named after him. (The *USS Forrestal* saw service in both Vietnam and the first Gulf War.) Forrestal instantly understood the significance of that moment for the reputation of the Marines. He turned to Smith and said: "The raising of that flag on Suribachi means a Marine Corps for the next 500 years."

Forrestal decided he had to have the flag as a souvenir, but when his request reached Chandler Johnson, the colonel spat, "To hell with that!" He was determined to keep it for the Marines. With an undignified race on to be first to grab the flag,

Johnson craftily decided that a much bigger replacement flag was called for. One was quickly located from a large landing craft just off the beach. Significantly, this flag had itself been rescued from one of the ships sunk at Pearl Harbor.

So it was that Captain Dave Severance, and six men from Easy Company's second platoon walked into history. Like Lieutenant Schrier's men before them, they worked their way up the hill with great caution, reaching the summit around noon. A large iron pipe was found to serve as a flagpole, and stones were piled up to hold the heavy pole in place. Near the summit was Associated Press photographer Joe Rosenthal. On an impulse, he went over to record the scene. He was still preparing his equipment when the flag was raised by six Marines. Rosenthal instinctively pointed his camera and clicked the shutter without even checking the shot in his viewfinder. Thus, in one four-hundreth of a second, the most famous American photograph of the war was taken. At the time, no one could possibly have grasped the significance of this particular moment. No one cheered. After all, it was just a replacement flag. The men of Easy Company returned to the fighting, their task complete. Of the six who raised the flag, three would subsequently die in the continuing battle to capture the island.

Rosenthal sent his roll of film off on a flight to Guam, a thousand miles to the south. Here it was developed and printed up, passed through army censors, and finally reached the desk of John Bodkin, the local Associated Press picture editor. It was his job to decide which shots were worth transmitting back to the bureau in America. Bodkin knew immediately he had a shot in a million. "Here's one for all time!" he told his staff. Sure enough, within two days of the shot being taken, it was on the front page of almost every American paper. Its arrival on picture desks was timely. At that moment, Iwo Jima was currently the most written about hot spot of the entire war, and public interest was massive. Rosenthal's shot became an icon, and prints were sold in their millions, to be framed and placed on workplace or living room walls, next to shots of sons and fathers in uniform. The image even appeared on 137 million postage stamps. After the war, a huge statue based on the photograph became the U.S. Marine Corps memorial in Washington.

Perhaps the same worldwide fame would have greeted Louis Lowery's shot of the first, actual, raising of the flag, had it reached newspaper picture desks first. But it didn't. Army shots always took a much slower route back home than those of commercial news organizations.

Kuribayashi and his high commanders had been correct in assuming the American public would be shocked by Marine casualties. They were. Within two days there had been more casualties than in the entire five-month campaign at Guadalcanal, in the South

Pacific, earlier in the war. It was unquestionably the American military's costliest operation so far. But the picture of the flag being raised less than a week into the campaign seemed to offer a major vindication. It said, quite incontrovertibly, that whatever their losses, the Marines at least were winning.

But that was only part of the story. Suribachi may have been the most strategically useful spot on the island, but its conquest was mainly symbolic. Another month of slow, agonizing, fighting dragged on before the Japanese were wiped out. Of the 21,000 men under Kuribayashi's command, only 216 were taken prisoner. The last two of these surrendered in 1949, when they found a scrap of newspaper reporting on the American occupation of Japan. They had kept themselves hidden in the maze of defensive tunnels inside the mountain for almost four years, pilfering food from U.S. army supplies to keep from starving.

The American casualties were also horrific. Few of the Marines who landed on the first day escaped unscathed. Altogether nearly 6,000 were killed, and over 17,000 were wounded. Kuribayashi's men had sold their lives with at least one or two American casualties. Survival seemed a matter of pure luck. Lloyd Keeland, caught up in the initial bombardment on the first day of the landing, fought for 36 days, although he was injured several times. He survived a night-time sword attack, waking up to hear a Japanese soldier attacking the man next to him. On

137

another occasion, he stood talking to a soldier who was shot in mid–conversation. After the battle, on a troop ship home, Keeland was haunted by nightmares of combat, one time waking to find he was strangling the man in the next bunk.

But the battle had served its purpose. Japanese fighter planes no longer harassed the American bombers that passed over the island. In the final months of the war some 2,400 damaged *B-29s*, which would otherwise have crashed in the sea, were able to land at Iwo Jima. The 27,000 U.S. airmen on board these huge bombers were saved from a near certain death.

The destroyer of worlds

The Manhattan Project, 1939-1945

Imagine the scene. Marooned in a research laboratory bunker hidden away in the desert, a group of scientists are concocting a strange experiment involving a bomb and the splitting of atoms. They are tampering with the very fabric of the universe itself, in an ultra-secret operation known as "the Manhattan Project". It is the middle of the night, and thunderous rain and howling winds lash the landscape. The soldiers sent to guard the scientists are in a state of high agitation. Some have overheard that the explosive device they are about to detonate is so powerful it could actually set the atmosphere on fire, incinerating all life on Earth.

The chief scientist, a tall, wiry-looking man called Oppenheimer, is chain-smoking, his inquisitive face tense with anxiety. He knows that when the experiment begins he will unleash the most powerful force in history. Oppenheimer is so unsure of what will happen he feels like a deep-sea diver under a huge depth of water, crushed by the weight of his responsibilities. The laboratory clock ticks away the final seconds of the countdown. Scarcely breathing, he raises a trembling hand to press the firing button, and takes a giant step into the unknown.

Outside, a good 9km (5 miles) away, the experiment springs into terrible life. The steel tower the bomb perches on is vaporized in an instant, and the desert beneath is scorched to glass. Night turns to day. It is as if the Sun has suddenly appeared with a colossal roar and mighty rush of wind. The brightness slowly fades to be replaced by a vast, billowing mushroom cloud of fire and smoke that reaches 12,000m (40,000ft) into the sky. Oppenheimer staggers out of his bunker and stands transfixed, overawed by his monstrous creation. He mouths the words of the Hindu *Bhagavad Gita*:

"I am become Death
The destroyer of worlds."

It sounds like an old black and white horror film, but it all happened. The place was Alamogordo, New Mexico. The date, July 16, 1945.

Robert Oppenheimer, then 41, was the leader of a team of scientists who had just constructed and detonated the world's first atomic bomb. The Manhattan Project had been an enormously complex and costly undertaking. Oppenheimer's team had three major problems. They had to create material to make a bomb, ensure it worked, then perfect a method of delivering this weapon to its target.

Starting with an initial budget of $6,000 in February 1940, this had escalated to $2 billion by the summer of 1945.

Getting the project started had been difficult. Even today, most people are baffled by the processes of atomic physics. Sixty years ago, the subject was completely alien. Scientists bidding for government funds would explain, for example, that each atom of uranium contained 200 million volts of electricity. Officials would greet such information with open-mouthed disbelief or even scorn. Only a letter to the U.S. President from the world's most famous scientist, Albert Einstein, eventually persuaded the U.S. Government to begin funding research into an atomic bomb.

By 1945 those working on the project included some of the most distinguished scientists from America, Canada and Britain. Most significantly, Oppenheimer's team also contained several refugees from Nazi Germany, Fascist Italy and other countries in occupied Europe. Among them were Niels Bohr, Enrico Fermi and Lise Meitner: three of the world's leading nuclear pioneers.

Since the beginning of the century, it had been known that powerful forces lurked within atoms. During the 1930s, scientists in both America and Germany had discovered the process of nuclear fission – where atoms are split apart to release energy. It soon became clear that such a process could be used to create an immensely powerful bomb. But only very few materials are suitable for fission. One is uranium 235, a substance obtainable from uranium ore. Another is plutonium, an entirely man-made material, produced inside a nuclear reactor. Acquiring even small amounts of both substances requires a costly, difficult and time-consuming process, involving massive amounts of electrical power. Both uranium 235 and plutonium are such powerful explosives that a sphere of either material the size of a large orange would produce a detonation equivalent to 20,000 tons of TNT – then the most commonly used explosive in shells and bombs.

The process of developing such a dangerous weapon was tricky. Some of Oppenheimer's team referred to their experiments as "tickling the dragon". But due to the skill and caution exercised by these world-class scientists, there were no fatal disasters during development. By the summer of 1945 the Manhattan Project had developed two kinds of bomb. One, known as the gun-type, would produce a nuclear explosion by firing a small piece of uranium into a larger piece. The other kind, known as the implosion type, fired several high-explosive charges into a plutonium core. In terms of factories, research and development labs, national resources and manpower, Oppenheimer's operation almost matched the scale of America's car industry. Despite employing 600,000 people, it was all top secret. Vice-President Harry Truman only found out about the

Manhattan Project when he became President, after the death of Franklin Roosevelt in April 1945.

What drove the American government to fund such a vast enterprise was the fear that their German and Japanese enemies would produce a similar weapon before they did. Once the fission process had been discovered, it was only a matter of time before someone produced an atomic bomb. But, fortunately for the world, Germany and Japan never really got close to developing a workable bomb - although the Allies didn't realize this until the war was over. Hitler's rabid anti-Semitism had led to the exclusion of immensely gifted German-Jewish scientists from German universities. Indifferent to the consequences, Hitler remarked: "If the dismissal of Jewish scientists means the annihilation of contemporary German science, we shall do without science for a few years." Although German nuclear physicists made essential discoveries during the 1930s and 40s, they were hampered by lack of funding. Some, fully aware of the evils of their government, falsified results to delay development. In 1943, just to make sure, British commandos destroyed a German laboratory in Norway, where atomic research was being carried out. The Japanese, similarly, lacked both the funding and resources ever to stand a serious chance of developing their own weapon.

Oppenheimer himself was fascinating, if not

entirely likable. He was tall, gaunt, and had a mischievous, pixie-like face. In many photographs it looks as if a playful quip is about to spring from his lips. But he could be crushingly unpleasant too – humiliating colleagues in lectures and discussion groups with biting sarcasm. In lesser mortals such conduct would be dismissed as despicable, but with Oppenheimer, people made allowances. Before the war began he established a reputation as one of the greatest scientists of his age. Despite the flaws in his character, he managed to build a brilliant team of physicists at the California Institute of Technology. He did much the same with the Manhattan Project. As an American Jew, he was particularly driven to produce such a weapon before the Germans did.

The breadth of his intelligence was astounding. His scientific studies encompassed both the infinitesimally tiny – atomic particles – and the astronomically vast – black holes. And Oppenheimer didn't stop there. Along with positrons and neutron stars, he also had space in his brain for French literature, ancient Greek, music, art and politics. His politics brought him no end of trouble. Many of his close family and friends, including one ex-girlfriend, were actively left wing and even communists. This was not unusual in America in the 1930s, especially among more liberal-minded academics and students. Oppenheimer was never a communist himself, but his remarkable career was nearly stalled on several occasions by government officials who had come to think of communism as some kind of infectious disease of the mind. They saw Oppenheimer as a security risk, fearing he would betray atomic weapons secrets to Soviet Russia.

By the time the bomb was ready to use, Germany had been defeated. But Japan was still fighting on fiercely, even though she had no hope of winning the war. In April, 1945, U.S. troops had landed on the Japanese island of Okinawa and fought for 82 days against fanatically determined resistance. America's leaders feared an invasion of the Japanese mainland would cost upwards of half a million American lives. The bomb was now ready, so they decided to use it. First, an ultimatum was issued to the Japanese government, warning of "the prompt and utter destruction" of their country if they did not surrender. It was debated whether or not to provide a demonstration to the Japanese, to let them know what the bomb could do. But this was rejected as impractical. The industrial city of Hiroshima, in the south of Japan, was chosen as its first target. One reason for its selection was that it had been barely touched by previous bombing raids, so it would be easy to determine how much damage had been caused directly by the atomic bomb.

The crew of the *B-29 Superfortress, Enola Gay*, stationed at Tinian air base in the Mariana Islands in the Pacific, were chosen to deliver it. "The bomb you are going to drop is something new in the history of warfare," they were told at their mission briefing. "It is the most destructive ever produced." Only a few of the 12 strong crew actually knew the exact nature of the bomb, and among them was weapons specialist Captain William Parsons. He had been sent directly from the Manhattan Project to oversee the mission. Parsons persuaded his commanding officer to let him finish assembling the bomb once they were in the air. The previous day he had watched four *B-29*s crash on takeoff at Tinian. Such a crash with a fully activated atomic bomb would have wiped out the entire island in one blinding flash.

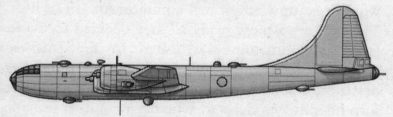

Bomb bay door: bomb stored here

A *B-29 Superfortress*, similar to *Enola Gay*

So, dangerously overloaded with her sinister cargo, *Enola Gay* lumbered off the runway at Tinian, just missing running into the sea. Flying alongside were two other *B-29*s packed with cameras and scientific instruments. It was 2:45 on the morning of August 6.

Fifteen minutes into the 2,400km (1,500 mile) flight to the city, Parsons clambered down a steel ladder into *Enola Gay*'s bomb bay. Here he gingerly inserted explosive charges into the bomb, which had been given the codename *Little Boy*. It was now fully assembled. A few hours later, just as the Sun was coming up over the North Pacific, Parsons made a final trip to the bay. Here he replaced three green plugs in the bomb with three red ones. *Little Boy* was now armed and ready. Pilot Colonel Tibbets chose this moment to inform his crew they were carrying the world's first atomic bomb.

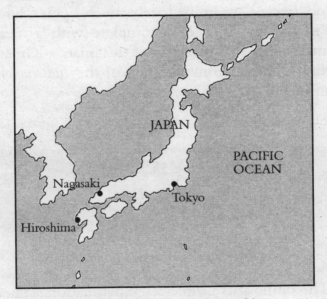

Map showing Hiroshima and Nagasaki, targets for the U.S. atomic bombs.

At 8:12am, *Enola Gay* began its bombing run. The sight of three tiny, silver *B-29*s high above Hiroshima caused little consternation below, and the city went about its early morning business as usual. In the glass nose of the aircraft, bombardier Major Thomas

The destroyer of worlds

Ferebee peered through his bomb sight, calling out small directional commands to Tibbets. The plane was heading directly for the Aioi bridge in the middle of the city. The bridge formed a distinctive T-shape, linking an island in the Ohta river with the city either side of its banks.

At 8:15am the bridge appeared directly in the lines of Ferebee's sight. The bomb was released from the plane. *Enola Gay*, immediately much lighter, lurched up in the air. *Little Boy*, complete with a message from the ship that delivered it to Tinian – "Greetings to the Emperor from the men of the *Indianapolis*" – plummeted to earth.

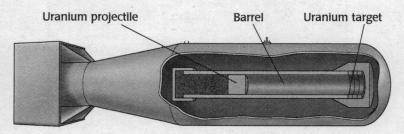

Uranium projectile   Barrel   Uranium target

The *Little Boy* atomic bomb, dropped on Hiroshima

The bomb had a three-stage detonation sequence, to guard against premature explosion. The first switch was triggered when it left the plane. The second was activated by air pressure when it reached 1,500m (5,000ft). The third, which would set it off, was operated by an on-board radar set to register 576m (1,890ft) above the ground. This was considered the height at which it would do the greatest damage.

Little Boy was a uranium gun-type bomb - different in design from the one that exploded at Alamogordo. Such a bomb had never been tested. It was possible it would not even work. But it did work - very well indeed.

At 8:16am, 43 seconds after it had fallen from the *B-29*, *Little Boy* exploded above a hospital, some 250m (820ft) off target. Instantaneously, with a blinding flash of light, the air was superheated, scorching the surrounding area to 3,000°C (5,400°F) - more than half the temperature of the surface of the Sun. Buildings and people simply vanished. In some places, shadows were all that remained of some Hiroshima residents. Their outlines had been caught on a wall or pavement for the fraction of a second before their bodies were vaporized. Birds dropped from the sky in flames. Further away, buildings were flattened, and people caught in the open were turned to charcoal statues, their fingertips glowing with eerie blue flames. A mile or so from the explosion, a train full of commuters was flung away from the track like a discarded toy. In those first few seconds, perhaps 80,000 people were killed. Then, as if this was not enough to suffer, air rushed back to replace that blown away by the initial blast. This created a hurricane-force tornado that sucked people and rubble into its swirling, dark heart.

High above, once they had recovered from the shockwave that tossed their plane like a cork on a wave, the crew of *Enola Gay* gazed down in awestruck wonder. Navigator Theodore Van Kirk noted that the city looked like a pot of boiling, black oil. The tail gunner described it as, "A bubbling mass...with that red core." Two-thirds of the city had been destroyed. When the fires died down, a strange black rain of ash and radioactive dust fell. In the weeks and years to come, another 80,000 Hiroshima residents would die of radiation poisoning.

That same day, the Americans called on Japan to surrender. A broadcast from the President warned of "a rain of ruin from the air, the like of which has never been seen on this Earth". But the Japanese were too stunned to react. Hiroshima had been so utterly annihilated, accurate reports of its fate could not be sent to Tokyo. When news did finally reach Japan's leaders, it was dismissed as a wild exaggeration. On August 9, another bomb was dropped, this time on the city of Nagasaki. It was a plutonium implosion-type device – the same kind tested at Alamogordo. It had much the same effect as the Hiroshima bomb, both in the damage it caused and the number of people it killed.

Still, powerful Japanese leaders, especially the war minister General Korechika Anami, argued that the war should go on. But eventually, Emperor Hirohito intervened to stop the fighting, declaring, "The time has come when we must bear the unbearable." Even then, army officers tried to stage a coup, with the intention of continuing the war. It failed. Anami

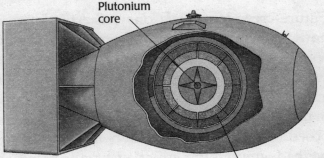

Plutonium core

Layers of high explosive, aluminium and uranium, which are fired into the plutonium core

The *Fat Man* atomic bomb, dropped on Nagasaki

committed ritual suicide, together with scores of other high-ranking soldiers who could not bear the shame of defeat. Fighting stopped on August 15. On September 2, Japanese government ministers went aboard the *USS Missouri*, anchored in Tokyo bay, and signed the documents of surrender. It was six years and a day after the Second World War had begun.

The dropping of atomic bombs on Hiroshima and Nagasaki were two of the most significant events of the war. At the time, the decision provoked heated debate among America's military and political leaders. Sixty years later, that debate still continues.

Some American generals were matter of fact about the whole thing. "I'll tell you what war is about..." said Major-General Curtis LeMay. "You've got to kill people, and when you've killed enough, they stop fighting."

The destroyer of worlds

Future president and one of America's most famous generals, Dwight Eisenhower, disagreed strongly: "The Japanese were ready to surrender, and it wasn't necessary to hit them with that awful thing." Admiral William Leahy, another high-ranking military commander, was even more vociferously opposed to the bombing: "...in being the first to use it, we had adopted the ethical standards common to barbarians in the Dark Ages."

Surprisingly, an argument for using the bombs came from the Japanese themselves. One leading politician, Hisatune Sakomizu, was quite clear about it: "If the A-bomb had not been dropped we would have had great difficulty to find good reason to end the war."

But for ordinary American soldiers the bombs were a fantastic release. Paul Fussell, then a 21-year-old officer preparing for the invasion of Japan, now a history professor, recalled: "When the bomb dropped and news began to circulate that the invasion of Japan would not, after all, take place, that we would not be obliged to run up the beaches near Tokyo assault-firing while being mortared and shelled... we cried with relief and joy. We were going to live. We were going to grow up to adulthood after all."

Alias "Uncle Ricardo"

The hunt for Adolf Eichmann, 1945-1961

When Adolf Eichmann organized the Wannsee Conference in January 1942, Germany was at the height of her power. But, during that year, the course of the war turned against her. By early 1945 it was obvious even to the most fanatical Nazi that the war was lost. Many who did not cherish the prospect of suicide, or a fight to the death, planned for their escape. Among them was Adolf Eichmann. In a post-war world men like him would be held accountable for the war crimes and atrocities they had committed, and so the best solution seemed to be to adopt another identity. As the war ended millions were being killed in desperate battles, or in the daily air raids that pounded the cities of the *Reich* to dust and rubble. It would be relatively easy to pretend to be someone else – especially someone who had died.

Eichmann, more than most Nazi fugitives, had much to answer for. He had organized the mass transportation of Europe's Jews to the death camps. It was Eichmann who negotiated with the German railway managers a third class ticket price for all his "passengers", with a 40% reduction for train loads over 1,000. He too, with others, had organized the setting up of the extermination camps in the first place. He had wielded his power with sadistic relish. "Jewish death lists are my preferred reading matter before I go to sleep," he once told a group of Jewish elders, sent to negotiate with him.

As the war drew to its painful end, Eichmann adopted the identity of one "Adolf Barth", a *Luftwaffe* (air force) corporal. Like many Germans, both soldiers and civilians, he was anxious to be captured by the Americans or the British. The war in the East, where the Nazi conquerors had behaved with inhuman brutality, had cost the Soviet Union 20 million dead. Now they had pushed the Germans back to Berlin, Soviet troops were in no mood to show their enemies mercy.

Eichmann surrendered himself to the Americans at Ulm, on the River Danube. What he didn't expect was to be interrogated quite so thoroughly. After several sessions with American Intelligence officers, he sensed his alibi was unconvincing, and managed to escape from the flimsily secured camp where he was held.

Over the next month, in the chaos that followed the end of the war, Eichmann passed through several other detention camps, where he invented yet another false identity. This time he was a "Lieutenant Eckmann". By June, he was held at a work camp at Cham in the Bavarian forest, where he and fellow prisoners were ordered to rebuild the town.

Eichmann confessed to a German civilian, Rudolf Scheide, who was in charge of the rebuilding, that he was really Adolf Eichmann. Scheide had not heard of him, and told him brusquely that he did not care who he was. But other prisoners had come across Eichmann during the war, and they had some inkling of what he had done. When one of these men revealed to Scheide exactly who Eichmann was, he went at once to the American authorities. They prepared to arrest this prime catch when he returned from his day's work. But Eichmann had friends as well as enemies among the prisoners, and he was warned in advance. By nightfall he had fled, heading north into an area of Germany that was occupied by British troops.

It wasn't just the Americans who were looking for Eichmann. One Jewish survivor of the camps named Simon Wiesenthal had lost 89 members of his family during the war. Together with other Jews, he was now determined to track down the Nazis who had carried out these atrocities – most of whom had now vanished. Wiesenthal, another Austrian Jew named Arthur Pier, and others, set up documentation offices in Vienna and Linz, in Austria where they assembled files and dossiers on missing Nazis. Eichmann was at the top of their list. Wiesenthal was especially well aware of Eichmann's role in "the final solution", and was determined to bring him to justice. At the time, they did not even have a photograph to help identify him. But Wiesenthal guessed that sooner or later Eichmann would return to his hometown of Linz, or at least make contact with his family there.

The philosophy of the documentation office was a shrewd one. No one was to take the law into their own hands and kill any Nazis they uncovered. Their job was to report such men to the Allies. Pier and Wiesenthal decided the best way to smoke out Eichmann was to send a handsome young man to try to befriend his wife Vera, who was claiming quite forcefully that she was now a widow. A resourceful Polish Jew named Henyek Diamant was chosen. Initially repelled by the idea, he eventually agreed to try. But Vera Eichmann proved resistant to Diamant's attentions, and he discovered nothing from her.

Another plan was called for. Eichmann was a notorious philanderer, and Diamant was asked to befriend some of his former mistresses. After several false starts he fell in with one of them, an Austrian woman named Maria Masenbacher. He told her he was a former Dutch SS man, who was too afraid to return home. Masenbacher and Diamant became lovers. One day, while going through an old photo album together, he spotted someone he thought might be Eichmann. When he asked Masenbacher who it was, she became flustered and quickly turned the page, telling Diamant that it was a friend who had died in the war. Sensing he was on to something, Diamant phoned a contact in Linz who had known Eichmann personally. Sure enough, he was able to confirm that it was Eichmann in the photo. Diamant vanished, along with the photo. Now, at least, they knew what their quarry looked like.

Although copies of the photo were circulated, they produced no immediate result, and Eichmann's trail went cold until 1947. Then, the American intelligence service informed Wiesenthal that Vera Eichmann had applied for a death certificate for her husband. She told the authorities that a Czech citizen had described how he had seen Eichmann shot to death during the liberation of Prague in May 1945.

Wiesenthal was immediately suspicious. If Eichmann was declared dead, his name would be removed from "Wanted" lists, and it would be extremely difficult to convince others to carry on searching for him. Sworn statements were found from Germans who had seen Eichmann alive in late May and June of 1945. Frau Eichmann's case collapsed when it was discovered that the Czech who had reportedly seen Eichmann die was in fact her brother-in-law. Many Nazis had escaped in this way. Officially declared dead, they had adopted new identities. Some had even remarried their supposedly widowed wives. Eichmann had been foiled, for now.

But help for Eichmann was on hand from other sinister quarters. In 1947, surviving members of the SS had used their formidable influence, and funds stolen from conquered territories, to set up a clandestine organization named *Odessa* (an acronym for 'Organization of SS Members'). They intended to help former Nazis accused of war crimes to escape from Germany and begin new lives in foreign countries. They soon discovered that South America was a prime destination. Not only was it the only continent on Earth untouched by the Second World War, but many of the countries there were run by dubious regimes, with no scruples about providing work for former soldiers whose brutality was legendary.

In early 1950, Eichmann was living in northern Germany near the city of Celle, raising chickens under the alias of 'Otto Heninger'. He had made contact with *Odessa* and was desperately saving his income to finance an escape. In May 1950, he was spirited away to Austria and Italy, and from there on to Argentina. He arrived in July with yet another alias – Ricardo Klement – and set about building a new life for himself. He was met in Buenos Aires by fellow Nazis, who found him work with a water company, prospecting for hydroelectric power plants.

But Wiesenthal now had friends among his former German enemies. He heard that Eichmann had been sighted in Rome, and was thought to be now in South America. Amazingly, this was confirmed when some other former Nazis approached Wiesenthal with a deal. They wanted to find Eichmann because they believed he had smuggled gold which they felt belonged to them. They suggested a collaboration.

Wiesenthal declined the offer, but not before he discovered that Eichmann had definitely gone to South America.

Time passed, and the world moved on… Many of Europe's surviving Jews emigrated to the new state of Israel, or to America. The Cold War between former Allies, America and the Soviet Union, created a new political climate. Former enemies were now considered useful friends. Even in Israel, the government was now more concerned with the hostile Arab states that surrounded it, than with hunting down former Nazis. In Linz, Wiesenthal kept up his surveillance of Vera Eichmann and her three sons, but they gave nothing away. Then, one day in the spring of 1952, the Eichmann family vanished.

Over in Argentina, Eichmann was doing very well. His skills as an organizer had led to rapid promotion, and within two years he had earned enough money to send for the rest of his family. His wife Vera received a letter from Eichmann, telling her that their "Uncle Ricardo" was prospering in Argentina, and that she should come and join him. Vera recognized the handwriting at once, of course. When they arrived, the boys, who had not seen their father for nearly eight years, when they were all very young, were told he was their dead father's cousin. They liked their Uncle Ricardo very much, and were thrilled when he married their mother. In due course, another son was born.

Wiesenthal, on the other hand, had fallen into a deep depression, as so much of his work remained unfinished. A doctor friend advised him to take up a hobby to distract his mind from his harrowing past and present failure. Speaking frankly to Wiesenthal, he warned: "How many victims were there? Six million? Well, you will be number six million and one unless you get yourself a real hobby, like stamp collecting."

So Simon Wiesenthal did just that. Then, in an extraordinary twist of fate, his hobby led him almost directly to Adolf Eichmann. One day in 1953, Wiesenthal attended a stamp-collecting exhibition in Innsbruck, and struck up a conversation with an old Tyrolean aristocrat, who invited him back to his villa. While they were looking through his stamp collection, the man began to talk about the Nazis, whom he despised. He remarked on how many former Nazis were regaining positions of power in the Tyrol, and then went on to say how well such men seemed to be doing in other countries too. Then, completely out of the blue, he fished a letter from Argentina from a drawer. A friend who had moved there after the war had written to say they had many former acquaintances out there. The letter went on: "Imagine who else I saw – and even had to talk to twice: that awful swine Eichmann who controlled the Jews. He lives near Buenos Aires and works for a water company."

Although he trusted his new friend, Wiesenthal

was too wily to let on that this information was of any particular interest to him. This man might write back to Argentina, and one way or another, Eichmann might hear that his trail was hot again. So instead, he just read the letter, and memorized as much as he could, writing it all down the moment he reached his hotel. Then Wiesenthal set about alerting the Israeli government and other Jewish organizations.

No one was interested. Eichmann had recently been reported sighted in several parts of the world, and there was no reason to suppose this claim was any more authentic. Disheartened, and now low on funds, Wiesenthal shut down his documentation office in Linz, and sent his files off to the *Yad Vashem Historical Archives* in Israel. But the one file he held on to was that of Adolf Eichmann. After that, he devoted his life to resettling refugees – both Jews and those fleeing from communist countries in eastern Europe. He worked as a director of schools set up to retrain people so that they could find work in their new countries.

Only in 1959 did Simon Wiesenthal pick up Eichmann's trail again. On April 22 of that year, he was reading the local paper and noticed that Eichmann's stepmother, Frau Maria Eichmann, had died. The paper listed Vera Eichmann as one of her surviving relatives. Someone, somewhere, obviously knew she was still alive, and probably with her husband. Wiesenthal cut out the piece and sent it off to several friends with contacts in the Israeli government. This time he provoked a reaction. It was enough to prompt the Israelis into reopening a search for Eichmann. Israeli agents came to see Wiesenthal, and he told them all he knew. Meantime, other Israeli agents had discovered Vera Eichmann was living with a German who went by the name of Ricardo Klement. From then on, Adolf Eichmann was living on borrowed time.

Further discreet inquiries revealed that the Eichmann boys were registered with the German Embassy under their real names. An address was also given. This further lead prompted the Israeli government to send three agents to Buenos Aires to set up house opposite the "Klement" family home. It now seemed obvious that they had found their man. Only it wasn't. Ricardo Klement was a dreary fellow, who shuffled through life and looked far older than he actually was. The lack of useful photographs of Eichmann also made a positive identification impossible. The best one they had was now twenty years old. But then Wiesenthal had another lucky break. In February 1960, Eichmann's father died, and the family gathered for the funeral. Friends of Wiesenthal photographed four of Eichmann's brothers – all of them had a distinct family resemblance. Now the Israelis watching "Klement" in Buenos Aires could match these new pictures with their man. Finally, and not without irony, it was an act of affection that eventually betrayed Eichmann. On March 21, 1960, he came home with a bunch of flowers for his wife. The agents knew he and Vera had married on March 21, 1935. It was enough to convince them that this was their man.

Adolf Eichmann was seized by Israeli secret service men, drugged, and smuggled aboard a passenger plane bound for Israel. There, behind bulletproof glass, he was tried in an Israeli court. There were many memorable and harrowing moments during the trial. Among them was the testimony of one prosecution witness who brandished a pair of tiny shoes. He explained to the jury that these pitiful leather scraps had been picked up from a pile of discarded footwear belonging to children murdered at Treblinka, one of the most infamous Nazi extermination camps in occupied Poland.

Wiesenthal was there in court to see the man he had devoted so much effort to bringing to justice. But, instead of some sort of demonic ogre, Wiesenthal was shocked to be presented with what he described as, "A frail, nondescript, shabby fellow... he looked like a book-keeper who is afraid to ask for a raise."

Eichmann was condemned to death by hanging – a sentence which was carried out in 1962. But, quite apart from other surviving Nazis, not everyone was pleased to see him executed. Even Simon Wiesenthal was uncertain. "When you take the life of one man for the murder of six million, you cheapen the value of the dead," he told biographer Alan Levy. Since Eichmann's death, fresh evidence has come up against him. Such evidence would have been brought against him in a court, but now never will be. Many people feel a life sentence is a far greater punishment than a quick death. Besides, as the war faded into history, some Nazi sympathizers began to deny the Holocaust had ever taken place. Real, living perpetrators of this most hideous crime, being forced to answer fresh accusations in courts of law, would have served as a reminder to the world that the Holocaust was not some fantasy nightmare. It really did happen.

From Technicolor to black and white...

In greatness or in evil, the chief characters of the Second World War – Winston Churchill, Franklin Roosevelt, Adolf Hitler, Joseph Stalin – dwarf almost all other political leaders of modern times. The set piece moments of the war – the Battle of Britain, Pearl Harbor, *Operation Barbarossa*, Stalingrad, the D–Day landing and the A–bomb attacks – are among the most significant events of the 20th century. The Holocaust, the Nazi destruction of the European Jews, is arguably one of the foulest evils in history.

Without doubt, it was the most horrific conflict ever fought. But, despite the scale of the war, its hardship and suffering, and its astronomical casualties, many people who lived through it, especially those from winning nations, look back on it as the greatest days of their life. For them, the battlefront campaigns, front-line or home front comradeship, wartime romance and eventual victory are all remembered in a blur of glorious Technicolor. The rest of their lives seemed to be lived out in dull black and white. One woman, Edith Kup, who worked for the RAF, expressed it like this: "It took me years to settle down to civilian life. I had changed and no longer spoke the same language as my family. Life seemed slow, dull and pointless. We had lived on the knife edge for so long, seen dreadful sights and lost many friends. Our responsibilities had been great, but it had been exciting and we had worked as close-knit teams. I wouldn't have missed it for the world."

Edith Kup worked in an operations room, helping to direct fighter aircraft to intercept enemy bombers. But those who actually fought in combat had even more vivid memories. Broadcaster and writer Ludovic Kennedy recalled his part in the hunt for the *Bismarck* as "the most exciting five days of my life".

But this excitement and comradeship was often bought at a terrible price. Many soldiers who had been through the war never spoke of their experiences to their friends and family back home. John Bradley was a navy corpsman (paramedic) attached to the U.S. Marines. He was one of the men who hoisted the Stars and Stripes over Iwo Jima. For the rest of his life he was haunted by the death of a close friend who had been with him on the island. Shortly after parting company from Bradley, this man had been seized by Japanese soldiers and slowly and grotesquely tortured to death over three days. It was a fate that could so easily have befallen Bradley himself.

For years after the war, Bradley would weep in his sleep, and kept a long knife at his bedside. Others took refuge in drink, to dull the grief they felt for fallen comrades, or to blot out memories of the terrible things they had done to other men. Many survivors of the war felt a heavy weight of guilt for having come home, when so many braver and better men – so they felt – had perished.

One small poem by John Maxwell Edmonds was popular with both American and British troops, who would engrave it on makeshift cemetery plaques close by their battlefields:

> *When you go home,*
> *Tell them of us and say,*
> *"For your tomorrows*
> *These gave their today."*

Those who fought the war, and who lost family and friends, liked to think they were fighting for a better tomorrow. The Cold War that followed, and the nuclear standoff between the United States and the Soviet Union, was a bleak end to the conflict. But the idea of a world controlled instead by the inhuman regimes of Nazi Germany and Imperial Japan is a truly haunting one.

Sources and further reading

The information in this book came from hundreds of different sources; books, websites, newspaper articles, radio and television documentaries.
The author would like to acknowledge and recommend the following sources which were especially helpful in the writing of this book:

General books
There are thousands of books on the war. Here are two particularly useful ones.
Time-Life's *Shadow of the dictators* (1989) gives a good introduction to both the rise of Hitler and World War Two, and is illustrated with evocative photographs.
The Reader's Digest *The world at arms* (1989) is a massive, highly illustrated and authoritative account of the war.

The first and final voyage of the *Bismarck*
Although there are several recent books which deal with the *Bismarck's* ill-fated voyage, *Pursuit* by Ludovic Kennedy (Cassell Military paperbacks, 1974) is a brilliant, even-handed and compassionate account.

The discovery of the Bismarck by Robert D. Ballard (Hodder and Stoughton, 1990) tells the story both of the voyage and the discovery of the ship by marine archaeologists 50 years later. It is full of fascinating photographs.

Cracking Enigma
Hugh Sebag-Montefiore's *Enigma - The battle for the code* (Weidenfeld & Nicolson, 2000) is a very readable history of this complex subject and contains first-hand accounts from surviving members of the crew of *U-110*.

Death of a salesgirl
Susan Ottaway's *Violette Szabo - The life that I have* (Leo Cooper, 2002) is a clear, solid and up-to-date account of this often romanticized figure.

Stalin's female "Falcons"
Information for this little-known subject was found on several websites and in an absorbing article by Jonathan Glancey in *The Guardian* newspaper, *The very few* (December 15, 2001).

The book-keeper's storage problem
The lost hero
Alias "Uncle Ricardo"
There are reams of books on the Holocaust.

Never again - A history of the Holocaust by Martin Gilbert (Harper Collins, 2000) tells the story in a readable, highly illustrated, comprehensive account.

Nazi hunter - The Wiesenthal file by Alan Levy (Constable & Robinson, 2002) is also a very accessible introduction.

John Bierman's *Righteous Gentile* (Penguin Books, 1981) and Danny Smith's *Lost hero* (Harper Collins, 2001) are two solid biographies of Raoul Wallenberg.

Roman Vishniac's *To give them light* (Viking, 1993) is a collection of photographs documenting the vanished world of Eastern European Jews before the war.

The war of the rats
There are two especially readable accounts of the epic Battle of Stalingrad: Antony Beevor's *Stalingrad* (Penguin, 1998) and William Craig's *Enemy at the gates* (Penguin, 2000).

"...like running through rain and not getting wet."
One of the most recent titles on the much-covered battle at Iwo Jima, James Bradley and Ron Powers' *Flags of our fathers* (Bantam Doubleday Dell, 2000) is a beautifully written but harrowing account, which may not be suitable for younger readers.

The destroyer of worlds
Jack Rummel's *Robert Oppenheimer: Dark Prince* (Facts on File Inc., 1992) is a gripping introduction to the Manhattan Project and its leading personality.

From Technicolor to black and white
The quote by Edith Kup comes from *The women who won the war* by Dame Vera Lynn (Sedgewick & Jackson, 1990).

TRUE
ESCAPE
STORIES

Paul Dowswell

Finally, the night had come to take a trip to the roof. Morris spent the day beforehand trying to curb his restlessness. What if the way up to the roof was blocked? What if the ventilator motor had been replaced after all? All their painstaking work would be wasted. The 12-year sentence stretched out before him. Then another awful thought occurred. The holes in the wall would be discovered eventually, and that would mean even more years added on to his sentence.

As well as locked doors, high walls and barbed wire, many escaping prisoners also face savage dogs and armed guards who shoot to kill. From Alcatraz to Devil's Island, read the extraordinary tales of people who risked their lives for their freedom.

Also from Usborne True Stories

TRUE SURVIVAL STORIES

Paul Dowswell

As he fell through the floor Griffiths instinctively grabbed at the bombsight with both hands, but an immense gust of freezing air sucked the rest of his body out of the aircraft. With the wind and the throb of the Boston's two engines roaring in his ears, he found himself halfway out of the plane, legs and lower body pressed hard against the fuselage. He yelled at the top of his voice: "Geeeerrrooooowwww!!!!", but knew immediately that there was almost no chance his crewmate could hear him.

From shark attacks and blazing airships to exploding spacecraft and sinking submarines, these are real stories of people who have stared death in the face and lived to tell the tale. Find out what separates the living from the dead when catastrophe strikes.

Also from Usborne True Stories

TRUE STORIES OF HEROES

Paul Dowswell

His blood ran cold and Perevozchenko was seized by panic. He knew that his body was absorbing lethal doses of radiation, but instead of fleeing he stayed to search for his colleague. Peering into the dark through a broken window that overlooked the reactor hall, he could see only a mass of tangled wreckage.

By now he had absorbed so much radiation he felt as if his whole body was on fire. But then he remembered that there were several other men near to the explosion who might be trapped....

From firefighters battling with a blazing nuclear reactor to a helicopter rescue team on board a fast-sinking ship, this is an amazingly vivid collection of stories about men and women whose extraordinary courage has captured the imagination of millions.

Also from Usborne True Stories

TRUE
SPY
STORIES

Paul Dowswell & Fergus Fleming

"In all your years of fame," Kramer explained delicately, "you have known some of the most powerful men in Europe. Would you consider returning to Paris now to mingle again with these influential gentlemen? And, while you're doing this, might you be able to keep me informed of anything interesting they might say?"

Margaretha looked curious but non-committal.

Kramer went on, "We could pay you well for this information – say 24,000 francs."

What are real spies like? Some, like beautiful Mata Hari, are every bit as glamorous as famous fictional agents such as James Bond. But spies usually live shadowy double lives, risking prison, torture and execution for a chance to change history.